Essential Principles for Fundraising Success

Essential Principles for Fundraising Success

An Answer Manual for the Everyday Challenges of Raising Money

G. Douglass Alexander and Kristina Carlson

JOSSEY-BASS
A Wiley Imprint
www.josseybass.com

Published by Jossey-Bass
A Wiley Imprint
989 Market Street, San Francisco, CA 94103-1741   www.josseybass.com

Jossey-Bass books and products are available through most bookstores. To contact Jossey-Bass directly call our Customer Care Department within the U.S. at 800-956-7739, outside the U.S. at 317-572-3986, or fax 317-572-4002.

Jossey-Bass also publishes its books in a variety of electronic formats. Some content that appears in print may not be available in electronic books.

Library of Congress Cataloging-in-Publication Data

Alexander, G. Douglass, 1946-
　　Essential principles for fundraising success : an answer manual for the everyday challenges of raising money / G. Douglass Alexander, Kristina J. Carlson.— 1st ed.
　　　　p. cm.
　　Includes bibliographical references and index.
　　ISBN 0-7879-7584-2 (alk. paper)
　　1. Fund raising—Handbooks, manuals, etc. 2. Nonprofit organizations—Finance—Handbooks, manuals, etc. 3. Proposal writing for grants—United States—Handbooks, manuals, etc. 4. Fund raising—Computer programs—Handbooks, manuals, etc. I. Carlson, Kristina J., 1964- II. Title.
　　HG177.A37 2005
　　658.15'224—dc22   2005011551

Printed in the United States of America
FIRST EDITION
HB Printing 10 9 8 7 6 5 4

CONTENTS

FIGURES, TABLES, & EXHIBITS

PREFACE

Raising money for a nonprofit organization is not an easy job. In our more than forty-six combined years of experience working with thousands of nonprofit organizations from start-ups to large internationals in virtually every state in the United States, we have seen many passionate people grow weary from fundraising's everyday challenges.

In 1999, we heard from one such professional who was tired of "reinventing the wheel." She called us and explained that she worked with a small nonprofit in Wisconsin. Her budget was small, but she really wanted someone to give her fundraising guidance. So she asked if the firm would provide fundraising counsel by e-mail. This was not something we had ever thought of doing, yet it made sense.

We agreed to be her online consultant. We gave what we thought was some very basic advice: build a detailed budget for your project, and make your website more donor friendly. Within two months she obtained a $65,000 gift.

At this point our proverbial lightbulb went on. There are more than a million nonprofit professionals who struggle with fundraising challenges every day, and many of them are dealing with very similar issues. And we both had known more nonprofits that we wanted to help but could not do so due to time constraints.

So we began to discuss how we could share advice and ideas in an efficient and affordable way. We brought together some of the industry's leading fundraising experts and with their help created the first Internet-based fundraising consulting firm: FundraisingINFO.com.

As part of FundraisingINFO.com, we created Ask Bee—a service that provides personalized answers to any fundraising question. Since we launched the site in February 2000, we have answered more than five thousand questions from thousands of nonprofit professionals and volunteers from around the world. We have gotten tremendous satisfaction out of this work.

The heartfelt questions sent by caring fundraising professionals and volunteers inspired us to write *Essential Principles for Fundraising Success*. One message that we hope it sends to those of you reading this book is that you are not alone. Many of your colleagues face some of the same fundraising challenges you do, and there are tested solutions for even your most difficult situations.

We hope you will find this book to be a useful and practical resource for improving your fundraising.

May 2005   G. Douglass Alexander
Atlanta, Georgia, and Water Valley, Mississippi   Kristina J. Carlson

ACKNOWLEDGMENTS

Like thanking people at an event, naming specific people who have contributed to this book is a dangerous thing to do. We will surely miss someone. Nonetheless, we are going to take that risk.

First, we want to thank Jossey-Bass for believing that this book would be of interest to nonprofit professionals. Second, this book would not have been possible without the experiences we have had for the past five years at FundraisingINFO.com. The investors and believers in our vision began with John Cay III, who wrote us the very first check to get us started and to pay the bills we had already run up. Ginger Barton Chakalall played a pivotal role in two ways: she created the first beta website, and she wrote the successful book proposal. The leaders of many fundraising consulting firms also played an important role not only as advisors but also as investors. Included in this group are Jimmie R. Alford, Leo P. Arnoult, Howard C. Benson, the Biggins and Mollsens of American City Bureau, George A. Brakeley III, Donald Campbell, the Carlsons of IDC, C. Ray Clements, Ben Dyer, Edith Falk, the Honorable Hank Goldstein, Bobbo Jetmundson, Nancy L. Rabin, George C. Ruotolo Jr., and Russell G. Weigand. Jay Toole was instrumental in advising about the formation of the Charter Partners, a group whose credibility and support have proven invaluable.

There are others who contributed in too many ways to name: Susan Boyette, David Brown, Bunky, Amanda Cavanaugh, Mike Goodman, Jim Hackney, Jerry Henry, David King, Del Martin, Linda McNay, Cheryl Mott, Missy Ryan, Larry and Loretta Shattles, David Shufflebarger, and Terry Stent. For those we left out, we apologize.

This book is dedicated to Be, Garland, Bob, and Ev:
the lessons you have taught us extend to
the fundraising world and beyond.

Essential Principles for Fundraising Success

INTRODUCTION:
PURPOSE AND OBSERVATIONS

Mrs. Leonard "Be" Haas was the ultimate fundraising survivor, working actively beyond her ninety-second birthday. She began providing fundraising counsel in Atlanta, Georgia, in the mid 1950s, and Doug Alexander began working with her in the late 1970s. Her expertise and influence impacted some of today's leading fundraising experts, including Howard Benson, founder and CEO of National Community Development Service; Claude H. Grizzard, Chairman Emeritus of Grizzard; and Del Martin, CEO of Alexander Haas Martin & Partners, among many others.

Be knew the secrets to fundraising success and shared them readily with organizations that sought her help. In fact, fundraisers in need of Be's assistance would come to her office in downtown Atlanta's Carnegie Building and dutifully tell her why they wanted to raise significant dollars. She would always listen attentively to the details of their unique situations.

Each case was indeed unique. Each had passionate causes, challenging financial circumstances, special board members, specific constituents, or some other aspect that made them different.

As a young consultant Doug would listen, under Be's guidance, to each unique circumstance and think that it warranted a breakthrough idea or approach that was going to be the easy, overnight solution to the particular organization's fundraising problem.

While Doug was busy thinking creatively, Be responded consistently to each case. She would say, "I have thought carefully about what you have said, and I think there are three things that we need to do to raise the money you want. The first thing we need to do is to develop a *case statement*, which explains why we need this money and how it will benefit the community. Second, we need to develop a campaign strategy that makes good sense and uses *sequential fundraising*— that is, securing some big gifts first—to build momentum. And third, we need to identify the strongest possible campaign leadership."

For the past sixty years, these three concepts have worked much better than new breakthrough ideas. Fundraising success requires the mastery of these three concepts.

Of course there is still much creativity and out-of-the-box thinking involved in fundraising. The creative process is used extensively to make case, plan, and leadership a reality, which is what makes fundraising both an art and a science.

Fundraising principles are both inviolable and adaptable. To be a successful fundraiser, you will need to use creative, out-of-the-box thinking almost every day to figure out how to convince your board members and others to follow proven, effective fundraising strategies.

In this chapter we answer the following questions:

- What is the purpose of this book?
- How should I use this book?
- How should I modify the ideas presented in this book for my organization's unique circumstances?
- Since fundraising is just like sales, and so many sales books have been written, why is a book on fundraising needed?
- With the economy, recent disasters, war and other circumstances, how will advice in the book help my organization continue to raise money?

What is the purpose of this book?

Essential Principles for Fundraising Success provides a fundamental approach to fundraising and practical answers and advice for everyday situations. The book will teach you how to develop a compelling case for support; motivate others to stick to a fundraising strategy built on effective principles; and inspire, recruit, and educate strong volunteer leadership.

We have used questions from fundraising professionals to demonstrate ways to apply fundraising principles in real-life situations while helping you to avoid common traps. Questions in each chapter are actual questions fundraisers have asked through our Internet-based consulting firm, FundraisingINFO.com.

How should I use this book?

You can use *Essential Principles for Fundraising Success* as a resource for questions related to specific topics, such as planned giving. You can also use it as your fundraising bible, with almost everything you need to know in one place. Rather than being an academic book, it is a practical resource to answer specific questions about important issues affecting you and your organization's ability to raise funds. In addition, you can read the book for guidance on what not to do. Examples include focusing on large corporations when you have no individual giving program; or relying only on special events to raise money; or chasing the ever-elusive foundation from far away.

How should I modify the ideas presented in this book for my organization's unique circumstances?

One of the common obstacles to success in nonprofit fundraising is the trap of uniqueness. By this we mean that fundraisers abandon all of the proven principles of fundraising because they view their current situation as totally unique. While virtually all nonprofits do indeed have different histories, different leaders, different communities, and so on, we have had success applying sound fundraising principles time and time again.

In fact, in 2004, Doug gave the keynote address to the annual meeting of NAYDO (the National Association of YMCA Development Officers) in Seattle. He asked the audience of seven hundred attendees, "How many of your organizations are unique?" Virtually 100 percent raised their hands. Although they were all YMCA representatives, they all had unique circumstances. Perceived uniqueness became the theme of the conference. Doug would pass people in the lobby the next day, and they would jokingly say, "But we really are unique." While every nonprofit's fundraising plans should start with a blank sheet of paper, an organization's uniqueness does not exempt it from fundraising fundamentals.

Since fundraising is just like sales, and so many sales books have been written, why is a book on fundraising needed?

There is a common misconception that fundraising is synonymous with sales. We have watched on numerous occasions as nonprofits have recruited people with a sales background to be their chief development officer or new major gifts officer. Board members and CEOs often think that selling harder will result in raising more money.

Pure sales—the ability to convince someone to buy something now, even if they might not need it—plays only a minor role in fundraising. In fundraising, no one has to give away money. Hiring a strictly sales-oriented person who has thrived on "closing the deal" can actually work against good fundraising principles. Fundraising is called *development* for a reason: the effective fundraising program develops connections with its donors before asking for money.

If you are a fundraiser, we understand that your boss and board members might expect you to be the hired gun. If this is the case, *Essential Principles for Fundraising Success* will present you with tools and techniques that you can use to educate others within your organization about all the elements of a successful fundraising program.

With the economy, recent disasters, war, and other circumstances, how will advice in the book help my organization continue to raise money?

Kristina worked for three years with Millard Fuller, the executive director and visionary for Habitat for Humanity International. She often remembers his simple yet insightful statement: "We have tried asking, and we have tried not asking, and we found that asking works better."

Fuller is right. Even in tough times, asking does work better. If you study statistics, which we discuss later in this book, you will see how much money donors give away each year, even after disasters, economic changes, war, and other adversities.

Yet we have encountered organizations that want to slam on the fundraising brakes whenever a circumstantial challenge exists. As a result, they send a message to their supporters that philanthropic support is only needed when times are good.

Our hope is that this book will provide you with advice and guidance that can strengthen your case for support, even when circumstances all around you suggest that the odds are against you.

CHAPTER ONE

PRINCIPLES OF FUNDRAISING: TIME-TESTED TRUTH

While we regard fundraising as both an art and a science (and while many people want to make it totally one or the other), there are certain basic principles that you can follow to be successful in fundraising.

In late 2003 and early 2004, we helped Boys & Girls Clubs of America develop an annual fundraising campaign built upon effective fundraising principles. They then tested the principles with about twenty of its local organizations. The staff and board leadership at many of these organizations embraced the ideas but struggled in their practice. Nonetheless, by committing to the principles and working hard to implement them, we saw dramatic, positive changes in their fundraising results. In total, the local organizations increased their annual fundraising by 150 percent in one year.

In this chapter we explain the principles of effective fundraising and answer the following questions:

- What are the principles of effective fundraising?
- Why do face-to-face solicitations produce the best results?
- Why should we focus our fundraising efforts on individuals?
- What does "money follows involvement" mean?
- How can challenge gifts solve most fundraising problems?
- Why must the board lead for others to follow?
- Why is personalization of fundraising solicitations important?

- Why should I involve volunteers in fundraising when I work more quickly without them?
- How does our organization present donors with opportunities?
- What is sequential fundraising?

What are the principles of effective fundraising?

We have nine principles that have worked for us in countless situations and campaigns. Whether directing capital campaigns for museums, hospitals, or universities; whether helping prep schools raise $100 million or coaching a brand new grass-roots group through its first $25,000; these principles have served as the foundation of successful fundraising campaigns. The nine principles are as follows:

1. Face-to-face solicitation is the most effective way to raise funds.
2. Individual giving, not corporate and foundation support, offers the greatest fundraising potential.
3. Money follows involvement.
4. Challenge gifts can solve most fundraising problems.
5. The board must lead for others to follow.
6. Make it personal.
7. Believe in volunteers.
8. Offer opportunities.
9. Practice sequential fundraising. Start at the top.

Why do face-to-face solicitations produce the best results?

Face-to-face solicitation is the most effective way to raise funds. Yet for some people it is the most difficult. A face-to-face meeting with a prospective donor enables the solicitor to make the strongest case possible for the request, answer questions that the donor might have, ask for consideration of a specific gift amount, and set up a next step with the prospect to obtain their pledge or check. One of the most important aspects of the personal visit is that the solicitor has sent a clear message to the prospect that this request is a serious matter and that it is personally important, since the solicitor is taking valuable time to meet with the prospect and request financial support.

Why should we focus our fundraising efforts on individuals?

Individual giving, rather than corporate and foundation support, offers the greatest potential for organizations to raise more money. Well over 80 percent of the money given away each year comes from individuals rather than corporations and foundations. For many inexperienced fundraisers, this is an eye-opener—it's easy to think immediately that corporations respond most generously to organizations that desperately need money.

What does "money follows involvement" mean?

People give money where they are involved. The Connectivity Matrix, discussed in Chapter Two, shows that the more connection that prospective donors have with your organization, the more likely they are to give you money. The more involved, engaged, and passionate your donors are, the more likely they are to give. This is a simple principle that works.

Doug experienced a good example of this concept in a campaign in which he was serving as the consultant. The High Museum of Art received a $12 million gift from John and Sue Wieland to name the new Renzo Piano designed pavilion. The original pledge to the campaign was $500,000, then grew to $5 million and eventually to $12 million to name the new facility. The gift increase was the direct result of the Wielands' continued work with the architect and with Michael Shapiro, the Nancy and Holcombe T. Greene, Jr. Director of the High Museum of Art. John served in the crucial position of building committee chair throughout the design and construction phase of the project.

How can challenge gifts solve most fundraising problems?

A *challenge gift* is a contribution offered by a donor on the condition that others contribute as well. The challenge not only provides a large gift to the effort but also leverages other giving and strengthens the "ask" by solicitors. In one very large campaign we worked on there were at least five different challenge grants through various phases of the campaign, including a "completion challenge" by the Kresge Foundation. (We explain how to creatively structure challenge gifts later in the book.)

Why must the board lead for others to follow?

This principle has stood the test of time, yet many nonprofits do not put enough emphasis on recruiting board members who are significant potential donors. As Be Haas would so bluntly say, "If your board is not going to give, why would anyone else give?"

We recognize that boards have different needs at different times in their history. A board for a start-up organization might look very different from that of a more mature one. But if a major campaign or substantial annual financial support is an organizational priority, recruiting and involving a strong fundraising board should also be a priority.

Why is personalization of fundraising solicitations important?

Personalizing a solicitation shows your donors that you know them and thus have a greater connection with them. Often, the more personalized the appeal the greater the gift. This is true not only for personal face-to-face solicitation but for direct mail, special events, planned giving, and telephone solicitations. This is also why media publicity can be one of the least effective ways to obtain funding. The lesson to be learned from following this principle is to strive for the greatest amount of personalization that is feasible. If you can visit a prospective donor in person, this is better than a phone call. If you can call a prospective donor, that is better than a letter. If you can send a letter addressed "Dear Jim," that is better than sending a letter addressed "Dear Friend."

Why should I involve volunteers in fundraising when I work more quickly without them?

Effective volunteers can be one of the best ways to raise money. Notice that we say *can be*. The securing of effective and dedicated solicitors is one of the great challenges that nonprofits face. The involvement and training as well as the natural ability that a good volunteer fundraiser needs are not common commodities; however, they are powerful tools.

Effective volunteers, unlike many busy staff, can get face-to-face meetings with major donors. The well-respected volunteer also gives tremendous credibility to the organization.

How does our organization present donors with opportunities?

When donors ask fundraisers the question, "Why should I give you any money?" fundraisers must respond with both an emotional and a rational appeal. Giving away money is an emotional process for most donors; it is also rational in that the donor wants to ensure the prudent use of her or his donated funds.

Every nonprofit in the world needs money. A case that focuses on need is weak and uninspiring. Show donors how to change the world or make a difference by investing in your organization, and you will make your case stand out from the competition.

What is sequential fundraising?

Sequential fundraising is the process of creating positive momentum for the campaign by trying to secure the largest gifts first, before proceeding to the smaller gifts.

All fundraising plans should have sequential fundraising as a crucial part of the strategy. Sequential fundraising enables you to measure how successful you are relative to your plan. It helps you set a watermark of giving for others to follow, and it offsets failure by showing early in the fundraising process how successful you are in securing the essential large gifts needed to meet your goal.

Summary

While sometimes difficult to apply, these proven principles serve as a framework for much of the advice given in this guide. We have seen them work time and again and know that they can work for you.

CHAPTER TWO

ESSENTIAL FUNDRAISING TOOLS: FOCUSING YOUR WORK

In the Introduction and in Chapter One, we introduced a time-tested approach to fundraising. Much of your fundraising success will depend upon your ability to educate others in your organization about these principles. The tools and techniques described in this chapter will provide you with ways to demonstrate and communicate these basics of effective fundraising. They will also help illustrate the difference between fundraising and development. In order to thrive in fundraising, you and your organization need to understand the difference and not rely on quick-fix strategies that become long-term nightmares.

Additionally, you can use these tools to position yourself as the chief development officer and avoid the "we-are-unique" trap or worse, the "we-are-really-unique" trap.

This chapter will answer the following questions:

- What is a Range of Gifts Table?
- How do I build a Range of Gifts Table for a capital campaign?
- Do these same guidelines apply for annual campaigns?
- What role does a Range of Gifts Table play in planning special events?
- If the Range of Gifts Table shows that we need four gifts at $50,000, how many prospects should we have for those gifts?
- If our Range of Gifts Table shows what we consider to be an unobtainable top gift, should we add more gifts at the bottom of the table?

- Should volunteers and donors be shown our Range of Gifts Table? Or is it a tool for staff only?
- What is a Gift Grid?
- What is the Hierarchy of Fundraising?
- What is the value of prospect research?
- What is the Connectivity Matrix?
- How is the Connectivity Matrix used?
- What other fundraising tools are essential?

Let's address each of these questions in turn.

What is a Range of Gifts Table?

A *Range of Gifts Table* (sometimes referred to as a *Range of Gifts Chart* or *Table of Investments*) is a written plan of action that shows the number of gifts your effort will need at various gift levels, ensures agreement on the fundraising process, and measures your progress as the fundraising unfolds. Though they are traditionally used in capital campaigns, every fundraising plan—whether an annual fund, special event, or capital campaign—should include a Range of Gifts Table.

The Range of Gifts Table shows the number of gifts your effort will need at various gift amounts. Traditionally, Range of Gifts Tables have been used in capital campaigns. However, they are very useful tools for other fundraising efforts including annual campaigns and even special events.

The general guidelines vary for building tables based upon what kind of fundraising effort is planned. We developed our guidelines based upon the review of many successful campaigns.

How do I build a Range of Gifts Table for a capital campaign?

The most successful campaigns start with a top gift that makes up about 20 percent of the goal. The next ten to thirty gifts make up 40 to 70 percent of the goal, and general gifts comprise 10 percent or less of the goal. These guidelines for building a table for a capital campaign apply whether the goal is very small or very large. See Tables 2.1 and 2.2 for examples.

Do the same guidelines apply for annual campaigns?

Different rules apply when making a table for an annual campaign, in which broadening the base of support is as important as raising dollars. Often with annual campaigns, there is not one lead gift but a number of lead donors who belong to your

TABLE 2.1. $2.5 MILLION RANGE OF GIFTS TABLE FOR A CAPITAL CAMPAIGN.

Number of Gifts	Size of Gift	Total at Level	Cumulative Total	Percent of Goal
1	$500,000	$500,000	$500,000	20
2	$250,000	$500,000	$1,000,000	40
4	$100,000	$400,000	$1,400,000	56
6	$50,000	$300,000	$1,700,000	68
8	$25,000	$200,000	$1,900,000	76
20	$10,000	$200,000	$2,100,000	84
35	$5,000	$175,000	$2,275,000	91
many under	$5,000	$225,000	$2,500,000	100

TABLE 2.2. $110 MILLION RANGE OF GIFTS TABLE FOR A CAPITAL CAMPAIGN.

Number of Gifts	Size of Gift	Total at Level	Cumulative Total	Percent of Goal
1	$25,000,000	$25,000,000	$25,000,000	22
2	$10,000,000	$20,000,000	$45,000,000	40
5	$5,000,000	$25,000,000	$70,000,000	63
15	$1,000,000	$15,000,000	$85,000,000	77
25	$500,000	$12,500,000	$97,500,000	88
30	$250,000	$7,500,000	$105,000,000	95
40	$100,000	$4,000,000	$109,000,000	99
many under	$100,000	$1,000,000	$110,000,000	100

highest gift club level. The five largest gifts will probably make up about 20 percent of the goal. The next ten largest gifts will make up approximately 10 to 15 percent, with the next thirty gifts also contributing about 20 percent of the goal. The next fifty gifts add about 10 percent, and the next hundred after that add 10 percent, with all remaining gifts making up about 20 percent of the goal. Table 2.3 displays this pattern.

What role does a Range of Gifts Table play in planning special events?

Creating a Range of Gifts Table for a special event can help you educate your organization's leaders and volunteers about the need to secure significant sponsorship dollars prior to relying on the public to buy tickets.

As we show in Table 2.4, even with a title or underwriting sponsor that gives 30 percent or more toward your fundraising goal, $50,000 will have to be raised

TABLE 2.3. ANNUAL CAMPAIGN RANGE OF GIFTS TABLE.

$2 Million Goal

Number of Gifts	Size of Gift	Total at Level	Cumulative Total	Percent of Goal
2	$100,000	$200,000	$200,000	10
3	$50,000	$150,000	$350,000	18
10	$25,000	$250,000	$600,000	30
30	$15,000	$450,000	$1,050,000	53
50	$5,000	$250,000	$1,300,000	65
300	$1,000	$300,000	$1,600,000	80
many under	$1,000	$400,000	$2,000,000	100

TABLE 2.4. SPECIAL EVENT RANGE OF GIFTS TABLE.

$250,000 Goal

Number of Gifts	Size of Gift	Total at Level	Cumulative Total	Percent of Goal
1	$75,000	$75,000	$75,000	30
2 to 4	$12,500–$25,000	$75,000	$150,000	60
8 to 10	$6,000–$8,000	$50,000	$200,000	80
many under	$6,000	$50,000	$250,000	100

from general ticket sales. Other sponsorship levels can be table sponsors for galas or hole sponsors for golf tournaments.

If the Range of Gifts Table shows that we need four gifts at $50,000, how many prospects should we have for those gifts?

If you will be involving volunteers and staff leadership in conducting face-to-face solicitations, you need to identify roughly two to three prospects for each needed gift. If you will be using telephone solicitations or other less personal methods, you will need many more. If you are conducting a capital campaign, you can also plan that you will need approximately one volunteer for every five prospects to be personally solicited.

If our Range of Gifts Table shows what we consider to be an unobtainable top gift, should we add more gifts at the bottom of the table?

Sometimes the building of your Range of Gifts Table can be an eye-opening experience, especially if you are undertaking a new and large fundraising effort. If the top gift seems unobtainable, we find it is helpful to create a table that relies on an increase in the number of smaller gifts, as this typically will show you that without a large top gift the goal needs to be reconsidered.

Once you have created a table with many smaller gifts making up for the lack of a large gift, review how many prospects you will need for each gift and how many volunteers you will need for each prospect. In other words, raising many smaller gifts will take many more volunteers or significantly more resources (if you plan to conduct solicitations by phone or mail).

This type of exercise usually helps an organization's leadership understand that if the top gift seems unobtainable, they might need to reconsider the goal.

Should volunteers and donors be shown our Range of Gifts Table, or is it a tool for staff only?

Once you have analyzed and developed the table, use it as an educational tool with your volunteers, staff, and upper management to help educate them about the gift sizes that will be needed to succeed.

Most people who are not involved in fundraising as their profession tend either to be optimists or pessimists when it comes to raising money. The pessimists think there is never a good time to raise money. They say things such as, "Donors are tired of giving," "We cannot keep going back to the same people," or "The economy is bad or will be soon." The optimists think there is plenty of money "out there," and corporations and others could give money and not even miss it. A well-thought-out and sound Range of Gifts Table can help bring a sense of reality to these two extremes.

What is a Gift Grid?

A *Gift Grid* is a tool that illustrates the interrelationships between the prospects and the solicitation techniques that might be most effective. It helps drive home the point that the larger the gift the more personal the solicitation strategy must be. It also shows how best to use certain fundraising techniques.

Each organization should develop its own definition of what a small, major, and mega gift is so that the grid can be customized to its constituency. Again, this is a good tool to use with your board development committee and others to help explain fundraising concepts that work and to develop strategies for your fundraising program. Tables 2.5 and 2.6 display different aspects of the Gift Grid.

TABLE 2.5.   GIFT GRID PART A: DEFINITIONS.

	Source	Unrestricted / Annual	Restricted
Small Gift	current income	$25–$999	$1,000–$5,000
Major Gift	income/ accumulated assets	$1,000–$25,000	$25,000–$1,000,000
Mega Gift	assets/estates	$50,000+	$1,000,000+

What is the Hierarchy of Fundraising?

The Hierarchy of Fundraising (HFR), shown in Figure 2.1, shows how a total fundraising program can be built over time. Annual support over a period of time is most often the basis for the growth of a fundraising program. Annual giving provides a base of donors, which will grow.

Your best prospects to give you money in the future are ones who have given you money in the past. This is a well-documented principle of fundraising. The ultimate goal for many organizations is to conduct a large, institution-changing capital or endowment campaign. The HFR shows that it is best to have received several major gifts and to have a strong annual fund before undertaking a large-scale capital campaign.

A corollary to this concept is that major gifts programs can be launched as a follow-up to a successful capital campaign. Many well-run capital campaigns will have more prospects at the end of the campaign than they had at the beginning.

The HFR also helps to illustrate that mature development programs are the ones that usually receive deferred gifts.

What is the value of prospect research?

There are many prospect research tools you can use to help make your fundraising effort more effective. *Prospect research* is based upon the famous bank robber Willie Sutton's method of fundraising. When asked why he robbed banks, Sutton replied, "That's where the money is." Thus it is with prospect research.

Your staff's time and resources are best spent with prospects who have both high donor potential and passionate interest in your organization. We have a whole chapter on prospect research later in this book, but for now you, like Willie Sutton, want to know where the money is.

Good research about a prospect can result in better and more effective solicitations. The more you know about a person's philanthropic ability, the greater your chances of securing a gift.

TABLE 2.6. GIFT GRID: PART B.

	Identification	Solicitation Involvement	Solicitation Method	Solicitation Relationship	Frequency	Motivator(s)
Small Gift	in-house file purchase list	minimal	mail phone event	impersonal	yearly or more	institution
Major Gift	past donors suspects	established relationships	face-to-face	peer (president, executive director, development officer, board member, volunteer)	every 3–5 yrs	institution/donor
Mega Gift	past donors life event inheritance sale stock	personal relationships strong feeling specific interest	personal evolves over time stewardship issue up front	one who donor trusts, admires, believes in	once	donor desire for change "payback" recognition passion for mission

FIGURE 2.1.   HIERARCHY OF FUNDRAISING.

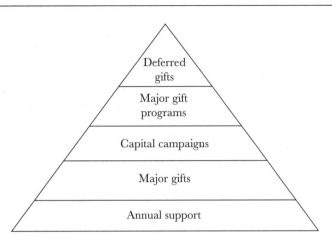

What is the Connectivity Matrix?

Another tool that further amplifies the principles of fundraising is the *Connectivity Matrix*, which is shown in Table 2.7.

The horizontal axis shows the degree of personal connection the prospect has with the nonprofit. The vertical axis shows the donor's ability to give.

The Bill Gates/Warren Buffet example in the upper-left quadrant represents a high ability to give but a low expectation of donation. Your best prospects for gifts are those who are involved in your mission, not wealthy people who could give money away and not even miss it.

TABLE 2.7.   CONNECTIVITY MATRIX.

Low Wealth–High Wealth	high wealth, no connection: no gifts (Bill Gates, Warren Buffett won't give if they're not connected.)	high wealth, high connection: many gifts (Here is where you want most donors.)
	low wealth, no connection: no gifts (If all your prospects are here, you still have work to do.)	low wealth, high connection: some gifts (These donors can make a difference if you are their number-one priority; consider planned gifts.)

Identified – Informed – Involved – Engaged – Passionate

How can we use the Connectivity Matrix?

As you are reviewing prospects with your fundraising committees, the Connectivity Matrix can be an effective tool to help evaluate your best prospects based upon both their ability to give and their likelihood of giving. It can also help you develop strategies to move your prospects farther to the right-hand portion of the matrix. Your largest donors will be those who have passion for your cause along with strong philanthropic capability (in the upper-right quadrant of the matrix).

What other fundraising tools are essential?

Every fundraising effort should use a fundraising software program to track prospects, donors, and results. These commercially available software programs have already considered the various tasks that need to be accomplished and the reports that are helpful during a fundraising effort. They will make it easier for you to measure the results of your fundraising efforts; produce appropriate acknowledgment letters and receipts to donors; track the history of relationships that your organization has; develop lists of prospects, volunteers, or donors; and identify prospective donors for your next fundraising efforts.

Because there is a wide variety of fundraising software programs commercially available that meet the budget needs of most nonprofit organizations, we see no reason for you to try and develop your own system. (See Chapter Thirteen for more information on software and technology.)

Summary

With a Range of Gifts Table, the Gift Grid, the Hierarchy of Fundraising, the Connectivity Matrix, and a good database system for managing your fundraising records, you will have the tools you need to educate and motivate your organization to follow the principles of successful fundraising effectively.

CHAPTER THREE

THE BOARD:
WHERE FUNDRAISING BEGINS

In our experience, board leadership and involvement is essential to success in fundraising. Yet almost daily we hear from fundraising professionals about the difficulty they are having with their boards. Boards tend either to be too involved in day-to-day operations or insufficiently passionate about the mission of the nonprofit.

Most nonprofits struggle with the proper and most effective role of their trustees in raising funds. This situation is equally true in both small and large organizations.

The successful fundraiser must regard the board as a valuable asset rather than a hindrance to fundraising success. Developing techniques and strategies to strengthen board involvement in fundraising can mean the difference between success and failure in a career. An important educational role of the successful fundraiser is to get board members to view themselves as advocates, donors, askers, and stewards of the organization.

The key to such an accomplishment is changing the perception that you and others might have of your job. One of the worst obstacles to fundraising success is the tendency to pigeonhole "fundraisers" as being totally responsible for raising funds with little or no support from anyone in the organization. Another is that you, the fundraiser, see yourself as needing to work in isolation because you do not trust that volunteers can be effective.

In order to be successful as a fundraiser, you must change this perception by being an effective educator of the staff and the board about what it takes institutionally to have a successful development and fundraising program. An important and practical way to begin this process is for the fundraiser to play a significant role in the identification, recruitment, and orientation process for all new trustees. The chief development officer should also be the key liaison with an active board development committee. The work of the committee is crucial to the success of all fundraising programs. Development committee members should be the most knowledgeable board members about fundraising. They should be knowledgeable about effective fundraising principles, such as face-to-face solicitations, as well as be leaders in the annual giving programs. An active, engaged, and informed development committee along with a development-oriented board-nominating process should be two factors that help ensure the priority of the fundraising program.

This chapter discusses how to get your board members to give and be involved in fundraising. It also shows how to use the nominating and development committees to improve your fundraising efforts as well as how to overcome board members' reluctance to ask for gifts. You will find answers to the following questions in this chapter:

- How do I convince my board members that each of them needs to make personal financial gifts to the organization?
- How should board members be solicited for gifts?
- I have been asked to do a presentation on fundraising for my board. What should I cover?
- As development director, my board thinks that it is my job to raise all necessary funds to balance our budget. How do I get my board involved?
- What are the key steps to forming an effective development committee?
- What are some strategies for helping a board member overcome reluctance to ask others to give?
- Does forming an advisory board help with fundraising?
- What should I do about a board member who uses our cultivation events to raise money for other organizations?
- Should we use consultants to help us with our board development process?

How do I convince my board members that each of them needs to make personal financial gifts to the organization?

One of the biggest impediments to 100 percent board giving is the perception of uniqueness. While many nonprofit organizations conceptually understand the importance of board giving, many never seem to be able to accomplish it because they view themselves as unique. Maybe they have board members whose employers give, so they see little need to give personally. Or maybe they have board members who are representing other segments of the community and are not being asked to give. Or the one we have heard most from smaller nonprofits is, "Our board is a working board."

A second impediment to board giving is often the method of solicitation. Board members often are asked so ineffectively that they do not think personal giving is important and valued. Handing out pledge forms at board meetings and telling every board member that they are expected to give something rarely returns good results.

A third and significant obstacle to healthy board giving is often the board recruitment process itself. We have seen many boards recruit new members with little thought to a recruit's past financial support of the organization and little effort to communicate clearly the expectation of financial support.

A good first step toward 100 percent board giving is asking the nominating committee of the board to consider only those candidates for board membership who are donors first. By developing this practice, the nominating committee can serve an important role in educating potential and current board members about the expectation for 100 percent board giving.

This can be done by sharing a written job description with each candidate that clearly shows personal giving as a responsibility of all board members. An effective technique to emphasize the importance of giving is to have new board members sign the job description to fully acknowledge their commitment to the tasks described.

How should board members be solicited for gifts?

Without question, the most effective method for soliciting board members is personal, face-to-face solicitation of each board member by a fellow board member or two. This can be done through the establishment of a board campaign committee that annually takes responsibility for the personal solicitation of each and every board member.

Personal solicitation means asking each board member to consider giving a specific amount that is in keeping with their personal financial abilities, rather than asking all board members to contribute the same amount. Some can give more, others less.

I have been asked to do a presentation on fundraising for my board. What should I cover?

We usually do not like to see staff members lecture board members on their responsibilities as board members. This job should be in conjunction with a development committee member. Your presentation could begin with an overview of last year's fundraising program: what worked and what did not. Then it could lead into a discussion of the plans for this year. In the discussion of the current year's plans, you could emphasize the need for volunteer involvement and board leadership in the fundraising program. Ask a board development committee member to lead the discussion on volunteer involvement.

As development director, my board thinks it is my job to raise all the necessary funds to balance our budget. How do I get my board involved?

Believe it or not, many people who serve on boards do not know what they are supposed to do and need to be educated about how best to serve the organization. Similarly, many people who are new to raising funds simply do not know how to ask for money. Knowing this, many development professionals mistakenly try to educate their board *en masse* about fundraising. They sometimes make presentations at board meetings about the importance of board involvement or compare their board's giving to the giving of other boards. Lectures in and of themselves cannot educate or motivate a board to become effective at fundraising.

The board has to take ownership of fundraising. This starts at the top with the board chair and other leaders. Trustees have to perceive fundraising as their responsibility. A general lecture about the importance of board involvement will not help the situation. If you are faced with a board that thinks it is your job to do the fundraising, every time you talk about the importance of their involvement you could be perceived as not wanting to do your job. So what does work?

First, keep in mind that board members are actually unique individuals with different abilities, skills, knowledge, and experience when it comes to raising funds. As such, board members will respond better to requests that are customized to their abilities and interests.

Start by identifying one board member who has the most potential as a leader and solicitor. Meet with this person one-on-one and discuss the importance of board involvement. Ask for the board member's help in educating other board members, perhaps by chairing or serving on the board development committee. As Exhibit 3.2 shows, the formation of a development committee is an essential step in effectively involving the board in fundraising.

What are the key steps to forming an effective development committee?

The formation of a development committee begins with finding one board member who understands the principles of fundraising and can articulate them to others. Educate this one person about the role of a development commit-

EXHIBIT 3.1. ROLES AND RESPONSIBILITIES OF TRUSTEES.

To further the goals of our organization, elected members of the board of trustees are expected to support the organization with their time, talent, and treasure:

- *Time:* The board of trustees meets six times per year. All trustees are expected to attend at least four of these meetings. In addition, all trustees will be actively involved throughout the year in some aspect of our organization's fundraising program. This most frequently will entail making calls to prospective individual, corporate, or foundation donors and identifying and cultivating potential supporters.
- *Talent:* Trustees will be invited to join the board because of their desire to enhance our organization and their ability to interest others in doing so with their gift support. In addition, each trustee will be asked to serve on at least one standing committee related to his or her special skills and interests.
- *Treasure:* All trustees are expected to support our organization through personal leadership gifts consistent with their means. At a minimum, trustees are expected to make annual gifts at the [dollar amount] level.

In addition, as capital projects are developed, trustees are expected to give serious consideration to supporting endowment and facilities projects. Each trustee will be encouraged to make provision for our organization in his or her estate plan.

Finally, as the stewards of others' gifts, all trustees are expected to meet their fiduciary obligations as trustees by ensuring that our organization has an appropriate financial management program in place.

In evaluating trustee performance relative to these areas of responsibility, the Nominating Committee is mindful of the unique contributions trustees can make. Whether they are in the areas of fundraising, advocacy, or program, the Nominating Committee gives due consideration to these contributions even when time constraints limit other participation.

tee. Together identify the characteristics you need, then think of specific committee members.

Work with this person to recruit additional committee members one at a time. Use the recruitment process to educate prospects clearly about expectations. You can customize the job description presented in Exhibit 3.2 to fit your organization's needs.

An initial committee of six to eight people would be appropriate. They should meet at least quarterly and perhaps more often when the committee is first formed. Once the group is operating effectively, expand the committee to ten to fourteen.

In a capital campaign, the development committee is often involved in selecting fundraising counsel, overseeing the campaign study process, and helping to set the initial campaign goal to be tested in the study.

EXHIBIT 3.2.   BOARD DEVELOPMENT COMMITTEE
JOB DESCRIPTION.

The development committee should meet regularly (not less than quarterly) and take an active role in the planning, execution, and evaluation of the fundraising programs. They must be sufficiently committed to lead the way in attracting funds—by both setting an example and enlisting the help of others. In addition to monitoring the progress of specific fundraising projects, the development committee should perform the following tasks:

1. Serve as a resource for the identification, cultivation, and solicitation of major prospects
2. Develop, with staff input, financial goals for each category of giving for the year and approve the written development plan
3. Assist in the identification and recruitment of volunteers and potential board members
4. Be responsible for seeing that board members are properly evaluated and personally solicited for their annual support, with a goal of 100 percent participation at a leadership level early in each giving year
5. Approve all fundraising policies (gift acceptance, planned giving, naming opportunities, and so on) and where appropriate obtain full board approval
6. At the end of each fiscal year, review the evaluation of the prior year's plans in light of actual goals achieved
7. When appropriate, participate on search committees for new development staff
8. Oversee initial planning for all capital, endowment, and special campaigns
9. Perform other such duties that would be consistent with membership on an effective development committee

A nonboard volunteer committee may be recruited to lead a capital campaign. This capital campaign committee often has board members and/or development committee members on it, but it is a temporary committee formed to conduct the campaign. It dissolves at the end of the campaign. The development committee, by contrast, should be a standing committee of your board responsible for ensuring ongoing support for annual operational needs during your capital campaign.

What are some strategies for helping a board member overcome reluctance to ask others to give?

There are many reasons someone might be reluctant to ask for money. They might not see themselves as having the necessary skills. They might have tried and failed.

They might think that they would have to give more to be an effective solicitor. Or they simply might have fear of rejection—the most common reason people resist fundraising.

An initial strategy for helping others overcome their reluctance to fundraising is to gently uncover the source of the discomfort. This can best be done through a face-to-face discussion.

As part of this process, discuss ways to involve the person in direct, personal contact with donors that does not involve asking for money. For example, they could get involved in personally calling and thanking donors for their previous gifts. Or they could be a support member of a solicitation team. This can be done by teaming the reluctant board member with an experienced solicitor, either staff member or volunteer. During the solicitation, the reluctant board member could be assigned the job of explaining the organization's mission and the importance of charitable dollars to the mission. Another team member would be assigned the actual "ask."

Once the reluctant board member has been involved in successful solicitations and heard firsthand the reasons donors support their organization, their reluctance might fade.

Does forming an advisory board help with fundraising?

Some organizations unfairly label their boards as "working" boards, "policy" boards, "representative" boards, or some other term that implies that the board can ignore one of its primary responsibilities: ensuring the financial stability of the organization. In cases where a label exists, it is common to see an attempt to form an advisory board to help with fundraising. We have seen some social service agencies go as far as to form separate foundations to avoid having to address fundamental issues with their boards. And we have seen organizations seek to form advisory councils because their development committees are not functioning.

The most important factor in forming an effective advisory board is to articulate clearly the expected role and contributions of the committee. Is the committee a technique to turn members into fundraisers or donors once they have agreed to be advisors, or do you really want their advice?

The process used to recruit initial members is important. A written job description (presented in Exhibit 3.3) should be created that clearly defines the role of council members. If you want the advisory council to raise money, say so up front. If you are unclear why you want an advisory council, develop an agenda for a year's worth of meetings. We have found that this exercise helps identify the role of the advisory council.

EXHIBIT 3.3.   ADVISORY BOARD JOB DESCRIPTION.

An advisory council member must do the following:

- Demonstrate a genuine interest in the plans and objectives of our organization
- Have influence and prestige in the community
- Be willing to devote time to the council as necessary
- Use his or her professional expertise as appropriate to help fulfill the plans and objective of our organization

Responsibilities of an advisory council member include the following:

1. Attend meetings called by the chair and contribute to the business at hand
2. Use personal and professional knowledge in support of the programs and plans of our organization
3. Be willing to advise the council chair and foundation board chair where appropriate according to his or her specialized knowledge
4. Be an advocate of our organization and act accordingly
5. Act as a community sounding board for pending or existing problems that could positively or negatively impact either [name of organization] or the foundation's programs
6. Assist in evaluating and cultivating potential donors as appropriate
7. Give annually to the organization at a level commensurate with your ability

What should I do about a board member who uses our cultivation events to raise money for other organizations?

We received an e-mail not long ago from a development director who was very frustrated with one of her board members. Her organization was hosting a lunch at a private men's club. The purpose of the lunch was to have the CEO present the organization's major community initiatives. Board members helped develop the invitation list and were asked to suggest guests who could ultimately make significant donations or represented companies that had a significant employee base that might utilize the new programs.

Without talking with the development director, one board member invited executive directors from other organizations in which he is involved and used the luncheon to introduce other guests to the missions of the other organizations.

Needless to say, we understood the frustration felt by the development director. However, it is not uncommon to have interaction among board members about their other charities. We recall one college retreat for board members where a member of the board was soliciting gifts for the local zoo capital campaign. Some of his fellow board members talked with him and put an end to that practice.

Having another board member, a peer, set things straight with the offending board member is a good approach to take if a board member is negatively affecting the activities of your organization. Another is to ask the board member, "How do you think having executive directors from other organizations at our luncheon will assist our organization and secure more support?"

Notice the response to your question. Maybe it planted a seed of second thought such that the incident will not be repeated. Just remember with all good volunteers there is occasionally some baggage. If the problem persists, talk with another board member about your concerns and see if they can help you address the issue.

Should we use consultants to help us with our board development process?

The right consultant focusing on the proper issues can be invaluable help to improving a board. The two consulting services most suited to board development are board audits and board retreats.

Board audits involve a review of the board's functions and result in a thorough analysis of your particular situation. An audit should generate of list of specific recommendations for your board to improve itself.

Board retreats with a fundraising perspective can focus on the most critical issues facing your organization. This intense interaction should produce several trustees who really "get it" and can take leadership roles when the retreat is over.

Our experience of having a speaker or consultant attend a regular board meeting to educate the board or get them excited does not yield much long-term success.

Summary

Rather than try to create ways to raise funds without your board, look for ways to renovate your board. A strong board that understands its role in fundraising is one of the greatest assets an organization can have.

Personalities can sometimes keep a board from seeing the processes that it needs to become more effective, which is why we have been developing a board renovation process that takes a comprehensive look at the role of the board. The process includes an examination of everything: the board's support for and understanding of the mission, adherence to bylaws, and use of written definitions of the roles and responsibilities of the board committees. This comprehensive approach enables an organization to focus on both its mission and its financial integrity. It has proven to be an excellent way to engage trustees in the life of the organization.

With some of the tools and ideas from this chapter, you can begin your own board renovation process by understanding that your job is first as an educator of others about fundraising, second as an active advisor to the board nominating process, and third as a facilitator of a functioning board development committee. These three focused activities will be the most important tasks to ensure the current and future health of your fundraising program.

CHAPTER FOUR

RESEARCH: WORKING SMARTER

Working smarter by using information to focus your fundraising efforts is the goal of prospect research. Prospect research has developed into a sub-profession for the fundraising industry. There is more information available today about donors than we could have ever imagined ten years ago. While prospect research did not begin with the Internet, the resources of the web have tremendously enhanced it. Trained prospect researchers can provide development officers with profiles of prospective donors that can be extremely helpful in solicitations.

Learning about a prospect's philanthropic history, financial capabilities, and personal interests can be important to the cultivation process for a major gift prospect. Good research can also help the development officer spend time wisely by focusing on donors who have the greatest potential to give. However, be aware that there is a limit to how much information you need to have before actually visiting with a prospective donor or adding them to your prospect list. The most important piece of information you can have on a prospect is not necessarily their wealth but their philanthropic history. The most successful fundraisers focus their energies on the wealthy and generous, not just the wealthy. Good prospect research can help you maintain focus and work smarter.

There are a number of good websites that list resources for conducting prospect research, and we could write a whole book about the mechanics of finding prospect information. While you will find some mechanical guidance in this chapter, we thought it was much more important to explain fundamentals and show the important role that good research plays in the total development process.

While the principles of research discussed herein are applicable to nonprofits worldwide, most of the resources referenced are applicable to research being done in the United States. Questions answered in this chapter include the following:

- What are the privacy and ethical issues related to prospect research?
- How do I build a prospect list?
- Where is the best place to start looking for grant makers for parochial schools?
- We are building an arts education program facility in France. Most of the students will be from the United States. Where should I look for funds?
- How can we do prospect research on a limited budget?
- What are the key sources of information for prospect research?
- Are there free or inexpensive avenues for finding information on average people?
- How do I know which screening services will help us identify our best prospects?
- How should we appeal to potential donors who were identified through a donor-profiling service?
- What is a reasonable target income and asset level that would produce a prospective donor at the $2 million range?
- As our list of prospective donors and donors grows, I am having trouble managing all the information. Do you have any suggestions?

What are the privacy and ethical issues related to prospect research?

There is a relationship between your donors and your organization. This relationship requires trust. If you collect information about your donors and do not protect that information or use it properly, you risk losing the trust of your donors.

The Association of Professional Researchers for Advancement (APRA) has studied the issues surrounding privacy and ethics. They break these issues into five main topics: confidentiality, accuracy, relevance, accountability, and honesty. You can find a copy of APRA's statement of ethics at www.aprahome.org. Meanwhile, here are some fundamental steps to ensure the ethical use of data:

- Organize the data.
- Use firewalls and up-to-date antivirus software to protect computers from hackers.

finding prospect information. While you will find some mechanical guidance in this chapter, we thought it was much more important to explain fundamentals and show the important role that good research plays in the total development process.

While the principles of research discussed herein are applicable to nonprofits worldwide, most of the resources referenced are applicable to research being done in the United States. Questions answered in this chapter include the following:

- What are the privacy and ethical issues related to prospect research?
- How do I build a prospect list?
- Where is the best place to start looking for grant makers for parochial schools?
- We are building an arts education program facility in France. Most of the students will be from the United States. Where should I look for funds?
- How can we do prospect research on a limited budget?
- What are the key sources of information for prospect research?
- Are there free or inexpensive avenues for finding information on average people?
- How do I know which screening services will help us identify our best prospects?
- How should we appeal to potential donors who were identified through a donor-profiling service?
- What is a reasonable target income and asset level that would produce a prospective donor at the $2 million range?
- As our list of prospective donors and donors grows, I am having trouble managing all the information. Do you have any suggestions?

What are the privacy and ethical issues related to prospect research?

There is a relationship between your donors and your organization. This relationship requires trust. If you collect information about your donors and do not protect that information or use it properly, you risk losing the trust of your donors.

The Association of Professional Researchers for Advancement (APRA) has studied the issues surrounding privacy and ethics. They break these issues into five main topics: confidentiality, accuracy, relevance, accountability, and honesty. You can find a copy of APRA's statement of ethics at www.aprahome.org. Meanwhile, here are some fundamental steps to ensure the ethical use of data:

- Organize the data.
- Use firewalls and up-to-date antivirus software to protect computers from hackers.

organizations that are similar in mission to yours to see who their contributors are. The following two questions help illustrate this point.

Where is the best place to start looking for grant makers for parochial schools?

It is essential that you begin your research on the people who are associated with your schools: parents, alumni, and church members. Most of your support will need to come from grant makers associated with them. Do any of the parents, alumni, or church members own businesses? Do they sit on foundation boards or know people who do? These are your very best prospects for giving.

Build a list of donors to other causes similar to yours. People generally give to more than one charity if they are philanthropic. Once the list is compiled, ask your board and development committee to review the list and help to identify the best prospects on the list. Ask them to think about others that you might have missed that also belong on the list.

We are building an arts education program facility in France. Most of the students will be from the United States. Where should I look for funds?

Since the students will be from the United States, look for foundations that have interests in arts education and that show they will give to capital (since you want the money for the facility). In other words, since you will be educating U.S. students, you do not need to limit your search only to foundations that have international funding interests. Also, look for corporations (and their foundations) that have operations in France. Consider also individuals who have participated in your educational programs who might have an interest in travel abroad.

How can we do prospect research on a limited budget?

Prospect research is the combination of activities and systems that help to match a prospect's interests, goals, and giving ability with your organization's goals and funding needs. Prospect research is also preserving your organization's memory of donors and prospects over time.

Some prospect research activities charge nominal fees, but they do require time. For example, it does not cost anything to ask a board member to review a list of people with you and tell you what they know about them. But how long would it take for you to have every person in your database reviewed and discussed by a board member versus doing an electronic screening on the database? Electronic or computerized screening is a service whereby your database is matched against a national database of wealthy, generous people to see if there are any prospects hidden in your list.

Long before electronic screening existed, most capital campaigns would recruit volunteers to form prospect review committees that would help staff evaluate the campaign prospects and determine appropriate consideration amounts for each. This was usually done with nothing more than peer knowledge about a prospect. Sometimes it can still be an effective way to segment and qualify your prospect lists.

Additionally, researching phone numbers, addresses, and background information on individuals can be done with a good Internet connection and some time. (As of this writing, www.theultimates.com is a helpful resource for finding such information.)

What are the key sources of information for prospect research?

Everyone is going to have different favorite resources. Even though there is a host of fee-based services that can assist a development professional with research, we like to focus on the ones that are available for little to no fees, as these are the most accessible.

To find contact information, you should first record all the information you already have from checks, pledge cards, and other sources. Then you can use external sources to find the missing pieces. For example, you can use www.theultimates.com or www.anywho.com to look up phone numbers, zip codes, and so on.

Next stop should be a "power search" to see what information is available on your prospect. We like to use www.google.com for our power searches, but any search engine (www.dogpile.com or www.msn.com) will also work. When doing "power searches," conduct your search with quotation marks around the prospect's name. This will narrow your search. You might also want to try some searches with the prospect's name and the words *donation, contributor, donor,* or *gift.* After a good "power search" it is usually pretty clear what other resources you might need to use to complete your research. Here are some of our other favorite resources and research tricks:

- To get an estimate of someone's salary range, try www.salary.com. On the homepage, you pick a job category and a zip code. On the next page, define the job title. Choose "Create Basic Salary Report." The next page will show the results of your search.
- To find other career information, try using a news archive such as www.newslibrary.com. Newslibrary lets you search many newspaper archives at one time and you only pay for the articles you want to read.

- If the person you are researching is a lawyer or a doctor, two sites—www.lawyers.com and www.amaassn.org—can be very helpful.
- More and more property records are online. Tax assessors' offices maintain property records for citizens within a particular county. For the most part, the information available includes the name of the property owner, the address of the property, the address of the property owner if different than the property, the assessed value, the year of the assessment, and, if you are lucky, appraised and/or market value. In some states you can use a multiplier to approximate the market value from the assessed value. The tax assessor's office is usually an agency of the county government. If you know the county where the prospect lives, then search for that county's website. A few sites might ask you to pay a nominal fee, but it might be well worth it. Searching the property holdings of the corporate entities, with which your prospect is associated (found in the secretary of state's records), can also be helpful.
- For individuals involved with public companies, one of the best places to look for information is their company's proxy statement (DEF 14A). If they are an "insider" (board member, key officer, or major stock holder), then you can usually find information such as age, employment biography, number of shares held as of the date of the proxy, stock options granted, and other juicy tidbits. The best place to start, if you indeed know the company name, is www.sec.gov/. This is the Securities and Exchange Commission's (SEC) website that displays key SEC documents from public companies. Simply select the document and use your browser's Find function to search for a keyword or name.
- If you are interested in seeing if your prospect is an active political contributor, check out www.opensecrets.org.
- Ownership of airplanes might be a good indicator of wealth. Of course, not everyone who has an airplane is particularly affluent, but if they own a large jet it is worth noting. Also, if you combine ownership of an airplane with other wealth indicators, you begin to get a picture of the prospect's use of discretionary income. A good site for airplane information is www.landings.com, where you can search for certified pilots and owners of airplanes. Information provided is name of owner, address, and some details about the aircraft. You can also use a paid service such as www.knowx.com to do assets searches that will find airplane ownership, boat ownership, and real estate for a charge. There is then an additional charge to read the records found.
- Of course, one of the best ways to find other relevant data about a prospect is to visit with them and ask. If you want to confirm or find a prospect's birthday, there is a fun little site you can use, www.anybirthday.com
- Also, be sure to check with your local library to see what kind of resource books it has. Some might have directories of wealthy people, business directories, and

other helpful resources (which include the librarian who might be willing to schedule time to train you on how to use the library's resources). Also, if you are really going to focus your time and energy on research, you might want to consider joining the best-known prospect research discussion group, Prospect-L. To do so, go to groups.yahoo.com/group/PRSPCT-L/ and join the group.

Are there free or inexpensive avenues for finding information on average people?

The most inexpensive way we know of to collect giving information on average people is to get the annual reports on all the nonprofit organizations in your area and organize their donor lists. (This is free in that you do not have to purchase anything, but it will take a lot of time.)

Personal income tax forms are off limits, and this will not change. You cannot obtain credit reports on individuals unless they have applied for a loan from you or given you permission to view their credit report. One consistently reliable resource for finding some indication of the "average Joe's" wealth is through property record searches. The value of the property of anyone in the United States can be found in the county or township tax assessor's office. There are a few websites that list the counties that maintain their information online. One is homepage.mac.com/researchventures/.

Electronic screening is the most effective and efficient way to look at a large number of people quickly and determine who has the capacity for larger gifts. With electronic screening, your database of donors, volunteers, and supporters can be reviewed, electronically, very quickly. Some electronic screening services are specifically designed to find the "philanthropists" hidden in your database.

There are basically two kinds of electronic screening: one will help you identify major gift prospects; and the other will help identify prospects for increased giving through direct mail, telemarketing, and annual giving purposes.

How do I know which screening services will help us identify our best prospects?

When evaluating electronic screening services, first determine what you are trying to accomplish. Do you want to identify your best prospects for major gifts? Or are you looking to refine some of your direct mail and telemarketing efforts? Your fundraising objective should help guide your selection.

Demographic-based screening is good when you have a very large database (twenty thousand plus), and you are trying to segment it for direct mail or telemarketing. The information you receive from a demographic screening will tell you whether or not a donor has indicated wealth and lives in a wealthy neighborhood, or on a street that has expensive real estate. It does not tell you if your donor is in fact wealthy but whether or not your donor might be wealthy because of where they live, what car they drive, or other demographic factors. Some services take all of the factors and rate the most likely prospects for you.

Individual-specific screening also can be done on large databases, but the results produced are specific to your actual donors' wealth and philanthropy, not their demographics. For example, some individual-specific screenings will tell you which donors own privately held companies, which ones have given million-dollar gifts, which ones have real estate worth more than $500,000, and so on. Services that rely on individual-specific information are much more helpful in identifying major gift prospects.

Your selection should also be guided by your overall development strategy. A key question to ask yourself is how much information you can use immediately. In other words, if the screening service identified twelve hundred new major gift prospects for you, would you be able to conduct cultivation and solicitation activities with these twelve hundred in the next year, or would it take you some time to use all that information? If it is going to take some time, you might want to consider screening small segments of your database on a periodic basis instead of your entire database at one time. In selecting a screening service, look for one that will help you segment your database to produce the results you need, versus wanting to screen your entire database regardless of your goals (which helps them make more money).

Review the philanthropic data the screening service offers. When looking for major gift prospects, remember the best indicator of a donor's likelihood of making a major gift is his or her history of making major gifts.

How should we appeal to potential donors who were identified through a donor-profiling service?

This question came to us from a major university that had employed a company to perform donor profiling. The information the university received was broken down into potential for giving major gifts, annual gifts, and so on. This is a great example of one of the key differences between some of the screening services available. Some are selling data, as in this case. Others are helping organizations not only find the data they need but also helping them develop strategies for using the data. In this case, the university purchased data and little else. You need to go back to the company that provided the data and ask for their written recommendations on your next steps. If the data vendor wants to charge an extra fee for this, you should instead consider hiring an experienced fundraising consultant for a day or two to help develop a specific plan of action for the data.

Another step to take in a case such as this is to review the profiling information on those donors that were in the major gift category and compare it with your donor contact and giving information. If you have individuals who were identified as major gift prospects that also have had strong relationships with your university but have never been seen face-to-face, we would recommend that these prospects be contacted for face-to-face visits. If you have some major gift prospects with lesser relationships (gave once, came to one event), you should move them into a higher annual giving category with the thought that if they do, you can then put them in a future group for face-to-face visits.

The overall strategy should be to develop a short list of prospects who have the greatest potential and who can be contacted and cultivated for a greater relationship with your organization.

What is a reasonable target income and asset level that would produce a prospective donor at the $2 million range?

Assuming that the donor considers your cause to be his or her top philanthropic priority, then the donor generally would need a net worth of at least ten times the gift amount, or in this case, $20 million, to make a gift of this nature out of current assets or income. The person's age is also an important factor in determining willingness to give at this level with their assets. For example, an older person maintaining a modest lifestyle with no children could give a gift of $1 million even if their assets were less than $20 million.

Research provided to us by MaGIC (Major Gifts Identification and Consulting, www.majorgifts.net) shows that there are approximately 3.2 million people in the United States who would be considered "philanthropic" and have personal liquidity well over $1 million.

As our list of prospective donors and donors grows, I am having trouble managing all the information. Do you have any suggestions?

One of the biggest challenges we see prospect researchers facing today is managing the seemingly unending sources of information. In order to make prospect research as productive as possible, it needs to be built upon the following practices:

- A solid system for recording all donor gifts, contacts, and activities.
- A good database system for managing donor records, prospect information, contact information, and more.
- Annual goals and objectives for the research (such as finding a certain number of new prospects, identifying a certain number of major donor prospects

for solicitation, and so on). These goals and objectives need to be tied to the development program's overall goals. For example, if you are adding a major gift program this year, how many cultivation visits will you have with potential major gift donors? This should be the number of new major gift prospects your research should attempt to identify this year.

- A consistent set of resources used to conduct research. (Researchers should narrow the list down to the ones most helpful to their particular needs.)

Summary

Spend your time wisely. Use the tremendous resources of good prospect research to help you focus on those major prospects that can make a transformational difference in your organization. Direct your research time toward your development goals. Finding major donor prospects does no good if you do not have plans or resources to engage and solicit them. The main goal of prospect research should be to ensure that staff and volunteers spend their valuable time cultivating and soliciting the prospects who have the greatest potential to give to your organization.

CHAPTER FIVE

ANNUAL CAMPAIGNS:
THE BASIS FOR THE FUTURE

A successful annual fund program is the basis for the growth of all future development programs. Without success in building a donor base, it is difficult for an organization to conduct major, capital, or endowment campaigns. The annual fund should be viewed as a comprehensive effort that includes direct mail, telephone, event, personal and group solicitations, and other techniques.

Annual giving (sometimes referred to as the *annual fund* or *annual campaign*), is critical to funding the operating budgets of organizations both large and small. Annual fund programs are year-round efforts that raise money to balance the budget while trying to increase the number of donors.

One challenge of annual fund programs is presenting the need for operating support in a way that does not make donors think they are just funding salaries and overhead. Like all sound fundraising programs, the annual campaign should be led by 100 percent giving from your governing board.

In this chapter you will learn about how to grow your program from one that might depend solely on direct mail or events to one that effectively includes personal solicitations, recognition programs, and challenge gifts.

This chapter answers the following questions:

- What is the difference between an annual fund and an annual campaign?
- Do we really need to have volunteers conduct individual solicitations for our annual campaign?

- How should we set a goal for our first annual campaign?
- What materials are needed to prepare for an annual campaign?
- How do we emphasize the critical need for giving to the annual fund (operations)?
- What is an effective way to train volunteers, donors, and staff about the importance of both participation and total giving in an annual campaign?
- How can I convince my boss that we need to do fewer events targeted at corporate sponsors and do more to establish an annual campaign targeted at individuals?
- What steps should I take now to boost my direct mail efforts?
- What are some strategies for implementing an annual campaign in a small rural community?
- In small organizations with limited volunteer resources, is it recommended to combine an annual campaign solicitation with a capital campaign "ask"?
- Can we bundle our annual campaign solicitations with sponsorship solicitations?
- Should we have group solicitations as part of our annual campaign?
- What are the pros and cons of seeking multiyear commitments during an annual campaign?
- When is it appropriate to ask regular, consistent donors to upgrade their gift?
- What do you recommend as a base donation for our volunteers to request?
- How do I evaluate my existing annual campaign program to develop better methods next year and beyond?
- How do we inform our past donors that we are changing the time of year of our annual campaign?

This chapter also includes a sample job description for an annual campaign volunteer and a worksheet to be used in evaluating an annual campaign.

What is the difference between an annual fund and an annual campaign?

Generally, an *annual fund* is the money raised from several fundraising activities (direct mail, phone-a-thons, and personal and group solicitations) for purposes of operating support. Gifts to the annual fund are usually unrestricted and spent in the year in which they are received to cover the costs of operations, administration, and programs.

When the term *annual campaign* is used, it usually refers to a comprehensive effort that incorporates face-to-face solicitations of individuals. Annual campaigns are generally organized around a board campaign and a leadership gifts effort that both rely on volunteer involvement in conducting solicitations. Newsletters and other mailings can be a part of the annual campaign as they help keep your donors up-to-date about your organization's key activities and reinforce both the need for giving and the impact of donated funds. Figure 5.1 shows the general components and solicitation methods for an annual campaign.

Do we really need to have volunteers conduct individual solicitations for our annual campaign?

Volunteer involvement is what generally distinguishes an annual campaign from a general annual appeal. And we could ask rhetorically, "What would you rather have volunteers do?" Attend meetings? Listen to reports from staff, vote yes, and go home? Or maybe sign letters? Yes, it would be a waste of time to ask a board member who regularly gives $25,000 a year to your organization and is effective asking others to give at similar levels to do annual campaign solicitations asking for $500. This board member should probably be making personal visits asking for major gifts.

We recently worked with a youth organization whose board members are leaders in their companies and their community. The organization's chief executive officer believed that since he had such a "high-level" board, he could not expect them to take the time needed to make personal calls for the annual campaign. In fact, considering how busy they were running their companies, he was grateful they attended board meetings. The organization's annual campaign consistently raised less than similar organizations in the same community.

When we had an opportunity to meet some of the board members, we found that they were very involved in raising funds for other organizations but not the

FIGURE 5.1.   ANNUAL CAMPAIGN COMPONENTS AND SOLICITATION METHODS.

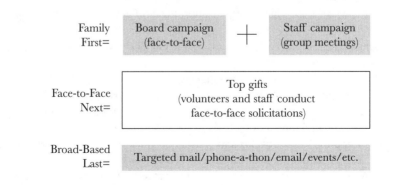

youth organization. When asked why they were not raising funds for the youth organization, most replied that they had not been asked to do so.

Involving volunteers in your annual campaign is a good idea for the following reasons:

- It greatly expands the number of people that can be personally asked, and personal solicitations will always produce better results than any other form of fundraising.
- Volunteers who are involved in asking others for donations typically increase their own gift amounts.
- If only staff members are making personal calls, there is a limit to the number of people who will be seen, and there is a risk that when a staff member is no longer employed, the organization's relationship with the donors will be lost.
- Volunteers who work in annual campaigns also will be better volunteers for future capital campaigns or major gift programs.
- It increases the number of people who understand and can articulate your case for support and creates ambassadors for you in the community.

Exhibit 5.1 presents a sample job description for an annual campaign volunteer.

EXHIBIT 5.1.   ANNUAL CAMPAIGN VOLUNTEER JOB DESCRIPTION.

Annual campaign volunteers have the following responsibilities:

- Believe that [organization] makes a significant difference in the community
- Believe that your actions contribute to the success of our organization
- Understand the importance of our campaign's success and articulate that importance to others
- Have confidence in our organization's plan of action for the campaign

Additionally, annual campaign volunteers will perform the following tasks:

- Attend campaign committee meetings
- Assist in the identification of the campaign's top prospects
- Make approximately five solicitations in person of top campaign prospects within the allocated time frame
- Attend the initial briefing and prospect review meeting as well as the training and prospect assignment meetings
- Attend report meetings and discuss the results of your solicitation meetings
- Make a personal leadership gift to the campaign

How should we set a goal for our first annual campaign?

If it is truly a brand new annual campaign, and there has never been any fundraising or donor base, then we think it is better initially to establish participation goals versus dollar goals, such as 100 percent board participation, 90 percent staff participation, and a goal for total number of other donors. As a part of this strategy, however, you should consider establishing giving levels and clubs to encourage gifts at more than nominal levels. Amounts such as $250, $500, $1,000, and $2,500 could be considered as possible levels. Be sure to involve your board and the leadership of your organization in setting the goals and uses of the fund. After your first year, use the first year's results to establish monetary goals for the next year.

What materials are needed to prepare for an annual campaign?

It is important to have the following records, documents, and materials in hand to prepare for your annual campaign:

- Current annual campaign written goals and objectives
- Annual campaign written plan including the following:
  - Calendar for current fiscal year and past two years
  - Annual campaign staffing organization chart
  - Annual campaign budget
  - Volunteer organization chart
  - Volunteer job descriptions
  - Annual campaign staff job descriptions, including performance expectations for employees in the annual campaign and performance evaluations
- Minutes of annual campaign meetings (if available from previous years)
- Accessible and up-to-date constituent database of prospects and past donors
- List of influential and affluent individuals in the organization's sphere of influence
- A system for producing monthly and annual gift reports
- Sample communications to constituents (direct mail appeals, reminders, acknowledgements for past two years)
- Sample of all annual campaign stationery and envelopes for past two years (if available from previous years)
- Solicitation analyses of each prior appeal
- Annual campaign case statement or brochures
- Phone-a-thon scripts
- Sample volunteer training materials
- Plans for donor acknowledgements and recognition

It can also be helpful to review your annual reports and donor reports for the past five years.

How do we emphasize the critical need for giving to the annual fund (operations)?

Many organizations have an annual fund that takes care of most program and operations needs. When special funds are formed to accept gifts for specific programs, donors might want to give to the programs rather than the general annual fund. One way to better position an appeal for the annual fund is to call it the annual campaign. (Some religious organizations name their efforts the annual stewardship campaign.) The message to donors of the annual campaign is that at least once a year, your organization will request and need to receive revenue for basic operating expenses. Even though the annual campaign will help pay for electricity bills and photocopy paper, office needs do not generally motivate people to make gifts.

In our experience, most donors are not going to get excited about supporting operations. Your annual campaign appeal needs to make the case for support by articulating the results of your operations and how you are fulfilling your mission with the assistance of philanthropic support. For example, if your organization is an association that supports churches, your case should answer how the association helps start more churches or how the association helps current churches get better educational materials. Or simply, your case needs to show what gets done because your association exists.

The annual campaign case should appeal to the donor's or the prospective donor's understanding of *value*. The case should appeal to an understanding, shared by writer and reader, that what the writer is asking for is so valued and special that it is very likely that the reader will want to respond positively with a gift or pledge of support. The content of the annual campaign case should reflect the nature of the organization and the urgency of the need. For example, if the organization is a theater, then the appeal might solicit funds in support of quality performances, mentioning how the arts stir the spirit and soul. And it might be written over the signature of the artistic director, an actor, or the chair of the board. If the organization is environmental in nature, it might outline a particular plight and program to remedy that situation. It could delineate the reasons why it is important to support the environment, appealing to individual responsibility and respect for others, and listing specific ways to help. It might even suggest certain gift levels.

What is an effective way to train volunteers, donors, and staff about the importance of both participation and total giving in an annual campaign?

Range of Gifts Tables are very effective training and education tools. They can show the need for gifts to be made at various levels, in addition to showing how every gift contributes to the goal. With a Range of Gifts Table, you can show that all gifts are needed but that gifts need to be made at larger amounts in order to reach the financial goal. The tables also help show that gifts from all are needed and that gifts need to be secured that represent equal generosity, not equal amounts.

Establishing giving levels and clubs can also help show the need for everyone to "join" (or participate) at a level that is consistent with their abilities.

How can I convince my boss that we need to do fewer events targeted at corporate sponsors and do more to establish an annual campaign targeted at individuals?

Many organizations hold too many fundraising events and spread themselves too thin. By going to the proverbial "well" too often for sponsorships, they squander the time they could spend fostering donor relationships and getting their annual appeal up to speed.

The antidote is to begin by conducting a thorough analysis of each event. Review how much each event costs versus how much each event generates. Be sure to include an allocation of any staff time in order to show "true costs."

Then consider that by doing so many events and focusing a lot of energy on corporate sponsorships, your organization is missing the most significant segment of philanthropy: individuals. Giving by individuals has consistently represented more than 70 percent of all charitable giving in the United States. When bequests are factored in, total giving from individuals increases to more than 80 percent of giving. This is the message to communicate to your president and others. The AAFRC Trust's publication, *Giving USA* (2004), has tremendously good statistics regarding the giving done by individuals versus corporations and foundations. (Visit www.aafrc.org for information.)

Once you have completed your analysis of the events and become familiar with the *Giving USA* data, arrange a meeting with your president to share what you have learned. Be prepared to suggest an alternative course of action: use the suggestions in this chapter to present a draft of a plan for an annual campaign.

What steps should I take now to boost my direct mail efforts?

Let's say your annual fund currently consists of a mailing that usually produces about $10,000. You want to boost this to at least $40,000 using board members to make phone calls and face-to-face solicitations in late November and early December. How can you accomplish this?

The following are some successful strategies that we have seen work for social service agencies, hospitals, colleges and universities, prep schools, arts organizations, neighborhood groups, and many other kinds of organizations.

1. Your board members should be donors before they ask others to give. So organize a board campaign (in which board members ask other board members for their contributions) for late September or early October. The goal of the board campaign needs to be 100 percent participation and should include a specific gift amount request and personal face-to-face solicitation meetings.

2. A challenge gift is a great way to encourage new and increased giving from donors. Identify someone (or a small group of individuals) who could provide a $10,000 (or higher) challenge gift that would provide $1 for every $2 of new and increased gifts to the organization this year. The challenge of $10,000, matched by a 1-to-2 ratio, would raise another $20,000; plus the $10,000 you have raised in years past, that would put you at $40,000. Plus, a challenge gift is easy for volunteers to discuss and creates a sense of excitement and urgency for donors.

3. To identify prospects for a challenge gift, you will need a small committee of board members (who have already made their own pledges) to work with you to review your prospect lists. If you have a board member who could provide the challenge gift, ask him or her first. Once you think you have some prospects for a challenge gift, you and your board members will need to solicit them face-to-face.

4. With your challenge gift in hand, start the rest of your campaign. While many people might not make their gift decisions until the end of the year, it might be difficult for volunteers to commit quality time between Thanksgiving and Christmas. It is best to do as many of your face-to-face solicitations prior to Thanksgiving as possible. (You will probably still be having some meetings after that time, but you would want to be closing any outstanding requests, not just beginning them, during this time.) You also want to plan your phone calls for earlier in the holiday season, rather than later. So if you are planning on sending a letter first, that needs to go out in late October.

What are some strategies for implementing an annual campaign in a small rural community?

In small communities, it is especially important to understand that raising significant dollars takes a system of identifying, involving, and soliciting the handful of individuals, corporations, and maybe foundations (if they exist) that are capable of giving much, much more than everybody else in the community.

You need to identify, cultivate, and solicit them in such a way that allows you to leverage anything they give with the giving of others. In our experience, individuals in small communities are careful about showing their wealth. They do not want to be perceived as being too different from everyone else. Research might be needed to identify them. Sometimes individuals in small towns make larger gifts in other communities, such as to their alma maters or organizations in towns in which they grew up or have family ties.

For example, we were once in a small, very rural town in Mississippi that did not have a traffic light but did have a very generous resident. He lives in a home that is comparable to others on his street. He does not drive a brand new car. Yet he made six- and seven-figure gifts to organizations in other parts of that state and throughout the South.

Additionally, our experience tells us these individuals do not want to be alone in their giving just because they are wealthy. Challenge and matching gift strategies are important. In other words, if your annual campaign goal is $50,000, you should try to identify some major donors who could give 30 to 50 percent of that. Then use their gifts as challenges or matches to others. For example, if you are doing an annual campaign, your challenge gifts could be used to match dollars given by new donors and increased gifts from current donors. Using a challenge-gift strategy is an effective way to say to everyone in the community that you need their support to meet the challenge, because even smaller gifts will be matched to make up a larger total. This same type of strategy can work for a special event: get one main large sponsor who helps underwrite the costs of the event.

In small communities, it is especially important that you set a watermark gift early in the campaign. A large gift early in the effort will help raise donors' sights and build volunteers' confidence.

In small organizations with limited volunteer resources, is it recommended to combine an annual campaign solicitation with a capital campaign "ask"?

A *dual "ask"* (or *joint "ask"*) is a type of a solicitation in which the donor is asked to consider a capital campaign pledge plus a one-year or current commitment to the annual campaign. When an organization embarks on its first capital campaign or has limited volunteer solicitors, it is extremely important to think through how annual campaign gifts will be solicited in the midst of a capital campaign. If there is not a sufficient number of volunteers to conduct an adequate number of annual campaign solicitations and capital campaign solicitations, then a joint "ask" makes sense.

Typically, a joint "ask" should be done by the capital campaign team as part of their normal capital campaign solicitations. When conducting a joint "ask," solicitors should have two campaign pledge cards: one for the capital campaign and one for the annual campaign. Prospects should be asked to complete both cards.

It is usually critical during a capital campaign that previous annual support donors continue their annual giving, and that their capital gift is above and beyond their normal annual gift. All capital campaign plans should be designed to protect ongoing annual support. Capital campaign volunteers need to be trained to explain the need for both capital and annual support.

The benefits of a joint "ask" are that you send a clear signal to donors that their ongoing annual support is important, and that their capital gifts are above and beyond what they normally give to the annual campaign. The solicitation for the annual gift and the capital gift protects the annual campaign and the yearly operating budget, a clear priority for most campaigns. The downside of this is that you might be asking for a six- or seven-figure gift and overly worrying about a few thousand dollars to the annual campaign. Another con is that if volunteers are involved in the dual "asks," you must make sure they have made annual and capital gifts themselves and are fully trained to get both pledges and to handle any objections that might arise.

Another less aggressive method is to train volunteers specifically to tell prospects that they will still be solicited for their annual gift and that the organization is counting on their support for ongoing operations. Be sure to make this point in all of your campaign communications, plans, and thank you letters.

Can we bundle our annual campaign solicitations with sponsorship solicitations?

There is nothing inherently wrong with bundling requests if it is clear that it is a comprehensive "ask": one for sponsorships and one for the annual campaign. This can be helpful to the corporate donor so that they do not suffer from the "every time I see you, you are asking for money" syndrome. To be successful with this type of approach, volunteers and staff solicitors need to be trained to present equally the case for the sponsorship and the annual campaign. Additionally, special effort needs to be focused on communicating with these donors throughout the year. Remember, by using a comprehensive "ask" you have cut down on the number of times you will be seeing the donor. So plan for a regular thank you visit that does not include a solicitation, and be sure to send regular newsletters and other communications.

Should we have group solicitations as part of our annual campaign?

Group solicitations can be effective if they are carefully planned and not a substitute for individual, personal "asks." They can also be helpful ways to solicit first-time donors.

In planning group "asks," try to get prospects with similar abilities in each group. In other words, try not to have a $10,000 potential donor sitting next to a $100 potential donor.

Kristina had a firsthand experience with this. She recalls sitting between two very wealthy individuals at a group solicitation meeting. Everyone at the meeting was asked to give the same amount. The amount seemed quite large to Kristina but probably small to the two individuals next to her. Frankly, it made Kristina angry to think that she was being asked to make a significant sacrifice while the other two were being asked for what was probably pocket change. On the other hand, if no amount had been suggested for everyone to give, she would not have known what level of participation was expected of her. Like many donors, she would not have wanted to give more than the two people who clearly had as much interest in the organization as she did and yet significantly more resources to give than she does.

When making group solicitations, it is helpful to have orchestrated one or two attendees to "speak first" about why giving is important and why they plan to give.

To prevent group solicitations from becoming mob solicitations, keep the group small, seat people with others of similar means, ask for specific action, and, if possible, give each person an individualized request letter or pledge card with specific gift amounts for the prospect to consider.

Finally, when planning group solicitations, keep modest expectations and be sure to plan your follow-up.

What are the pros and cons of seeking multiyear commitments during an annual campaign?

Some fundraising programs suggest soliciting multiyear commitments as part of an annual campaign. At first blush, this sounds like a great idea. If you can solicit people one time for their annual support and just collect the checks for the next three or five years, you will have more time in future years to cultivate and solicit more donors. Better yet, maybe you will not even have to worry about fundraising for the next few years because you will have completed all of your solicitations for the next few years in this year. If only it were that simple.

First, consider that this idea violates the proven marketing and fundraising principle that repetition breeds retention. Getting your message, successes, challenges, and opportunities in front of donors each and every year helps to build their commitment to your organization. If you only solicit donors once every five years, there is a good chance that by the end of a five-year pledge period, you are out of sight and out of mind. Or worse, you create a pledge collection problem. Additionally, there is the risk that you will turn what could be a growing donor relationship into an annual "bill" for their pledge.

The multiyear concept also ignores a fundamental goal of annual giving, which is to get people to start giving and then build the relationship and increase their giving over time. Most donors who are giving out of income tend to look at their giving on an annual or tax-year basis. In addition, annual solicitations make it easier to upgrade donors to higher levels, to maintain strong relationships with donors, and to involve donors in other activities at your organization (such as, well, fundraising). Finally, multiyear "asks" are generally associated with restricted giving, such as capital campaigns, special projects, endowment funds, and so on.

When is it appropriate to ask regular, consistent donors to upgrade their gift?

Let's say your organization has been conducting an annual campaign for two years now. Your next annual campaign will begin in September. Should you ask regular donors to upgrade their gift?

Each year, you can ask donors to consider upgrading their donations. Many donors at lower levels might not be able to remember whether they gave $40 or $50 last year. The important thing is to make sure you were appreciative of whatever amount they have previously given. One strategy that helps in asking for increased amounts is to secure a challenge grant for the annual campaign that encourages increased giving as part of the match of the challenge grant. This challenge can be a good rationale for why you are asking for more support. Another approach is to use giving levels (gift clubs) for annual campaign donors. When asking for an increase, focus on asking donors to join the next-highest level.

What do you recommend as a base donation for our volunteers to request?

You are about to conduct your first phone-a-thon later this month as a follow-up to a fundraising mailing sent two weeks ago. You will be calling individuals in your database, and most of them have not made a contribution in the past. How much should volunteers request?

Asking for a donation of $100 is a fine place to start. Train your volunteers to respond to any hesitancy to the gift amount with the suggestion that it can be paid as $25 four times a year or $10 a month for ten months. You might want to train your volunteers to offer lower amounts if $100 sounds too high for someone. "If you cannot make a gift of $100, would you consider a gift of $50?" And "any amount would be appreciated."

How do I evaluate my existing annual campaign program to develop better methods next year and beyond?

A two-hundred-year-old human services charity has, regrettably, allowed its fundraising program to languish in recent years. Their donor base is not nearly the size it ought to be, nor does it produce the money they need. The CEO and chief fundraising officer need to revamp and rebuild the annual campaign program. How can she evaluate her existing program to develop better methods in the future?

She can start by getting a complete history of the organization's annual giving and chart its progress over the previous five years. This analysis should provide a basis from which she can make projections. It is important to calculate not only total giving but also the number of donors and the total value of the top ten gifts received each year as a percent of total amount raised. The Annual Campaign Evaluation Chart in Table 5.1 shows other factors to consider when evaluating past years' campaigns.

In addition to these measurements, the chief fundraising officer will also want to analyze the techniques used to raise funds—special events, direct mails, board giving, and so on. This information should help her decide where to direct her efforts based on past results.

TABLE 5.1. ANNUAL CAMPAIGN EVALUATION CHART.

This worksheet can help you identify strengths and weaknesses in your annual campaign. To use it, you will need your last three years of fundraising data. For purposes of this worksheet, you should include only funds received from the specific fundraising activities you are evaluating.

Analysis Worksheet	Example Year	Year 1	Year 2	Year 3	Percent Change
Total dollars raised	$500,000				
Number of donors	1,250				
Average gift*	$400				
Number of new donors	200				
Number of increased donors	100				
Number of lapsed donors**	250				
Top gift amount	$75,000				
Top gift as percentage of total money raised	15%				
Total amount of top ten gifts	$290,000				
Top ten as percentage of total money raised	58%				
Number of face-to-face solicitations	15				
Total costs of all fundraising	$125,000				
Costs as percentage of funds raised***	25%				

*Dollars raised divided by number of donors

**Donors who gave last year but not in this year

***Total costs divided by dollars raised

And finally, to attain specific benchmarking comparisons, she might consider hiring a consulting firm to do a fundraising audit. This would help her identify key strengths and weaknesses in her program and aid in pinpointing some important next steps.

Once she has completed her evaluation, she should share her findings with the board development or fundraising committee, ask for their input on the analysis, and look for ways to engage them in discussions on how to improve future fundraising activities.

How do we inform our past donors that we are changing the time of year of our annual campaign?

You've inherited a lackluster annual campaign. Your first meeting with the foundation board was in December—two weeks after you became director of development. They have very little idea who their donors are. Their records are a mess. They usually send out their appeal in April. In addition to needing to update their donor files, they need to update their brochure as well. They need to shift their annual campaign to the fall. Yet some of their donors are used to getting a solicitation from them in April. How should you let donors know you are changing the time of year of the annual campaign?

Being new has its advantages and its challenges. In this case, the advantage is that you have a very compelling reason to focus on stewardship and to educate your board about the need for more stewardship activities. For example, you could send a newsletter or letter to past supporters updating them on what has happened since the last annual campaign. Announce in the newsletter that the annual campaign will kick off later in the year. Sending something now could help you clean up your list (with returns and bad addresses filtered out before you make an "ask").

Next, target your largest donors for face-to-face meetings—now. As a new director, you have an advantage in setting up meetings. You can say, "I would like to come meet you, introduce myself, and learn more about your connection to our organization." In setting up the meetings, be sure to mention that you will not be asking them for money at the meeting. Your goal should be to meet with the top ten donors to last year's campaign, thank them for their past support, and update them on the plans for the future. This way you will stay connected with them while you make plans for the annual campaign. It might also help you identify some potential volunteer leadership for your annual campaign.

Start working now on getting a challenge gift for your annual campaign. The challenge grant should be large enough to provide between one-third and one-half of the dollars you need to raise. You can then announce the challenge sometime before fall and use it in your annual campaign to encourage others to give by letting them know their gifts will be matched by the challenge grant.

Summary

The objective of every annual campaign should be to grow the donor base. That means each year you should be raising more money from more people and employing more proven fundraising techniques. The migration from staging events to conducting as much personal solicitation as possible in the annual campaign will create the foundation for your organization to raise significant funds through major gifts and capital campaigns in the future.

CHAPTER SIX

DIRECT MAIL:
HOW TO BUILD YOUR DONOR BASE

Historically, direct mail has played an important role in many development programs. It has allowed for the solicitation of large numbers of people in a relatively short period of time. Direct mail has also been used to secure new donors, upgrade lower level donors, and inform and educate an organization's constituents about key issues.

You will read in this chapter that direct mail is not a quick fix; it is a long-term investment that will produce results over time, not overnight. Direct mail is definitely a strategy in which it "takes money to make money."

Today new technologies are offering alternatives and enhancements to direct mail. Some organizations are finding that e-mail efforts are sometimes less costly while still being as effective as direct mail. Others are finding that direct mail can play a pivotal role in making e-mail efforts successful by, among other things, encouraging donors and prospects to visit a website and register to receive e-mails.

Throughout this chapter you will read about strategies for growing and building a direct mail program. You will also learn about the various kinds of mail programs and some successful ways to implement them. Finally, this chapter will also discuss our experience in upgrading donors who consistently respond to direct mail appeals to the best prospects for telephone or personal solicitations.

This chapter will answer the following questions:

- What is the difference between direct mail, acquisition mailings, and targeted mail?
- What are some keys to having a successful first targeted mail appeal?
- Where should we buy a list of new names?
- Is a brochure an important piece in a direct mail package?
- Is lack of personalization the "kiss of death"?
- Which is better in a solicitation letter: a moving story or a general description of an organization's programs?
- What should a second letter contain?
- Should information about an upcoming capital campaign be included in an annual fund donor acquisition letter?
- What is the average percentage of replies that a nonprofit can expect from a direct mailing piece?
- What is the average rate at which direct mail is opened? Do you have any suggestions for raising that rate?
- What is the best time of year to send out solicitation letters?
- How many letters constitute a sufficient test of a direct mail package?
- What is the industry time standard for keeping a one-time donor on your mailing list?
- How many letters must be sent to raise $50,000?
- How can mail be used to move donors to higher levels of giving?
- How do you manage the multiple goals of increasing average gift size and increasing the donor base, without increasing the budget?
- What is a good return on second mailings to new donors?
- Is it appropriate to involve board members in a direct mail effort?
- Should we sell or lease our mailing list to generate additional revenue?

What is the difference between direct mail, acquisition mailings, and targeted mail?

Defining your mailing efforts will most certainly help you produce better results. We use *direct mail* as an overall term to cover mailings that acquire new donors, retain current donors, and upgrade donors.

Acquisition mailings are generally massive and constant mailings (usually at a financial loss) to build one's donor file. These mailings are sent to people who do not yet have a relationship with your organization but who do match some demographic profile. Often the purchasing of lists is a part of large acquisition mailings. The goal of most acquisition mailings is to acquire new donors, not to break even. Acquisition mailings make money for an organization over time in that, once you acquire a donor, it is not their first gift but their subsequent gifts that eventually help turn a profit from the original acquisition mailing.

If resources are limited, acquisition mailings can be done with *home-grown lists*. You can build such a list by asking for prospect names from board members, researching your community to identify known givers and finding their connections to others organizations, and finding names of people who have some link to your organization. These activities can make acquisition mailing more similar to targeted mail than pure acquisition.

Targeted mail fundraising can be most valuable in retaining and upgrading donors (that is, persuading them to give more than their last gift). Targeted mail, which requires more personalization, is a relatively inexpensive way to reach your audience quickly, have total control of the message, and educate and inform them about your needs and their opportunities for giving.

What are some keys to having a good first targeted mail appeal?

First, make sure you have a good list to use in the mailing. A good list has minimal incorrect addresses. There are services that can electronically screen your list and correct any bad addresses. To find such a service, go to your favorite search engine on the Internet and search for "national change of address."

Second, personalize the letters as much as possible. Address letters to *John and Mary* or *Mr. and Mrs. Smith* as opposed to *Dear Friend(s)*.

Third, get your board involved in signing the letters and adding personal notes to letters being sent to people they know. Be wary of involving your board members in actually writing or editing the letter (unless they are direct mail experts).

Fourth, ask for a specific amount or range of money in the letter—tie the "ask" amount to past giving (if you are mailing to former donors).

Fifth, secure a challenge gift that will match any new dollars raised through the mailing. This way you can write that for every dollar that is given, your organization will receive one additional dollar (people love matching gifts).

Sixth, measure your results. To know which mailings are most effective you must track and evaluate them. Without evaluation, all mail is guesswork. The process is simple: how many people responded to a particular appeal and how much money did it raise? For each mailing, be sure to track the following:

- Total number of gifts received and amount given
- Number of donors by dollar category: who gave $25, who gave $50, and so on
- Percent of response: divide the number of responses by the number of pieces mailed

- The gift received most often (the dollar amount most often given [rather than the average gift, or the total dollars given by the number of gifts])
- Cost of mailing
- Ratio of income to expense: money received divided by money spent
- Written comments received from donors
- Which of the largest and newest donors are prospects for further involvement in your organization

Where should we buy a list of new names?

This is one of those questions that always make us a little uncomfortable, because we know that the answer we are about to provide and the answer being requested are going to be very different. Keep in mind that building a donor list by buying lists is a long-term proposition. In fact, many direct mail experts suggest that you should plan to lose money in your first year of mailing to a new list and that it might take two or three years to see real returns on a direct mail campaign that goes to a brand new list. In other words, launching a brand new direct mail campaign to a brand new list of names is not a good way to meet a budget deficit.

Is a brochure an important piece in a direct mail package?

Brochures might be necessary when mailing to a group unfamiliar with the organization. They are also helpful when you have a new service or program that you want to highlight. They are not as necessary when you are mailing highly personalized letters to current supporters. Also, longer letters can include all the information that is contained in a brochure.

One way that some organizations save on this expense is by printing bullet-point brochure-type copy on one portion of the business reply envelope or pledge card.

One alternative for you to consider is a test. In your next mailing, include a brochure with some letters and not others. See if you have any different results. For the test to really work, you will need to keep as many other factors the same as possible.

Is lack of personalization the "kiss of death"?

Some databases cannot produce personalized letters. This means you have to address all 350 appeal letters as *Dear Friends*. Such a lack of personalization does not have to be the kiss of death. Consider that you need the reader first to open the envelope before they will see the words *Dear Friends*. Personalizing the outside envelope is almost more important than personalizing the letter. Focus on addressing your envelopes personally. And if your mailing is small, such as 350 letters, you could ask your board members or volunteers to help personalize the letters with handwritten notes to people they know on your list.

Which is better in a solicitation letter: a moving story or a general description of an organization's programs?

You are about to begin a donor acquisition mailing to a list you purchased. You will use the list for one year and plan three letter mailings plus newsletters with information about your programs and services. Which type of letter should you send first? One member of your team prefers a letter telling the life story of one of your former residents (with permission), and another wants to send something that describes, in a more general way, your programs and services and how they help children.

Writing letters by committee is never fun, nor are office politics. Yet we all seem to get caught up in these kinds of activities. In this case, if you really did not want to be the one to decide which idea to use, and if you had a substantial enough mailing list, you might conduct a test to see which approach works best with your constituency.

In our experience, however, a good *impact story*, which highlights the results of your programs and services, is much more effective than descriptions of your programs and services. Many organizations have difficulty briefly describing their programs and services in a way that is immediately compelling to direct mail prospects.

Additionally, gifts made in response to direct mail are often made out of an emotional response rather than a rational one. Newsletters and annual reports can provide the rational background to the emotion. Direct requests will do better with an emotional appeal or a moving experience.

What should a second letter contain?

What should you say in your second request letters to those prospects and past contributors who have not sent checks as a result of your first letter? This depends on the nature of the mailing list. If this is a pure acquisition mailing, you might consider sending virtually the exact same letter. How many people do you think really saw your first letter?

Alternatively, you could do any of the following:

- Provide an update on the campaign, including how much has been raised from how many donors
- Provide an update on your program activities since the last letter

- Make a statement about how the person can help you reach the rest of the campaign goal in terms of dollars and number of donors
- Make a specific request for the person to become a donor and make a specific contribution
- Have or create a "deadline for response"

Do not make a specific reference to the fact that they have not given, or assume they got the first letter. There is a good chance they did not see the first letter.

Should information about an upcoming capital campaign be included in an annual fund donor acquisition letter?

We suggest that you write about your long-term goals, plans, and needs without mentioning the capital campaign. As much as possible, capital campaigns should be discussed with donors one-on-one long before they are published in acquisition letters. To combine the two messages might confuse readers about what kind of help you need—do you want help for the expansion or for the annual fund?

What is the average percentage of replies that a nonprofit can expect from a direct mailing piece?

We find this question impossible to answer accurately. The rate of response will depend on the quality of the list, the source of the list, the type of package mailed, and other factors.

With this in mind, we have seen some studies that suggest that acquisition mailings might produce response results as low as .5 percent and as high as 4 percent. With an acquisition mailing, however, the goal is to acquire as many new donors as possible at the lowest possible cost, not worrying too much about rate of return or cost per dollar raised. Mailing to former donors should produce response rates as high as 80 percent if the donors have given more than once.

In the end, however, we think it is much more important to measure your direct mail program against its strategic goals and its history rather than against industry averages that really might not apply to your specific organization's type, budget, or history.

What is the average rate at which direct mail is opened? Do you have any suggestions for raising that rate?

We do not know of any general statistic for direct mail opening rates. Most organizations (and businesses) measure this type of statistic in several ways: by looking at the dollars raised from a mailing; by conducting surveys (which can get expensive); or by enclosing information on a phone number to call, a website to visit, or a reply card to return, and then measuring the calls, hits, or cards received.

To increase the number of people opening your mail, keep in mind that the more personal you make the envelope or outside mail piece, the larger your readership will be.

People get so many flyers, envelopes with labels, and mail addressed to *Dear Friend* or *Dear Resident.* It is hard to stand out using similar techniques. However, an envelope addressed by hand to John Smith is a rare thing for John Smith to receive and thus will probably grab his attention. And with signature machines and other technology, giving envelopes a personal look is now more feasible than ever. They are still more costly than labels and printed envelopes but nonetheless possibly much more effective. Another more costly approach is to use real stamps versus metered postage.

There is one fundraising mechanism that can track opening rates: e-mail. With the right software, you can know who opened your e-mail, whether they opened any links in your e-mail, and whether they forwarded the e-mail to others.

What is the best time of year to send out solicitation letters?

We do not know if there is one best time for all organizations. In fact, many direct mail experts would say that one time is not enough anyway and that you should mail something to your donors at least six times a year. Traditionally, late November is a good time to mail, as many people are making or thinking about year-end gifts.

More importantly, though, you need to determine the best times for your program, which will require some testing. Try doing more than one mailing a year (if your budget permits) and see when you have the best results. Ongoing analysis of what you have done in the past is the best tool for helping to determine what you need to do in future mailings.

How many letters constitute a sufficient test of a direct mail package?

Your president wants you to test different appeal packages sent to members you are asking to renew. Each renewal mailing goes to about three hundred to five hundred people on average. Is that a statistically significant sample?

It is possible that this is statistically significant and that the information you will gather, combined with your instinct, will help you understand what is working and why. In fact, you can increase its significance if you can divide the group into three similar groups and send a different message to each group to see how it performs. The groups would have to have an equal number of donors, nondonors, lapsed donors, and so on to make such a test work.

Before taking any further action, you might want to ask why your president wants you to conduct these tests. Is the president looking for ways to be more involved in your fundraising activities? Would the president like to be better informed about the results of your activities? Are you meeting the financial needs of the organization? Is there a need for increased fundraising activities? Has someone on the board recently expressed dissatisfaction with the number of donors? Getting to the bottom of the president's suggestion might help you involve the president in your fundraising efforts in a more effective way.

What is the industry time standard for keeping a one-time donor on a mailing list?

In our experience, it is not much more than three years. But before you start relying on industry standards, take a look at the results you get when you mail a solicitation letter to one-time donors. Do you get better than a 1 percent return when you mail a solicitation to all of your one-time donors? How does this compare to mailing to nondonors? If you are getting a better rate of return from one-time donors than you are from nondonors, it is worth keeping one-time donors on your list for future mailings.

How many letters must be sent to raise $50,000?

You are planning to send personal letters to past donors asking them to join your major gifts club with a minimum gift of $1,000. While you only have about one thousand members of the major gift club now, you have access to a database of over one hundred thirty thousand past donors. What is the minimum mailing necessary to raise $50,000?

Unfortunately, there is no rule or formula as to how many letters must be mailed to achieve a $50,000 return. The only way you could accurately guess is to base it on the results of past mailings for your organization.

Conventional wisdom in membership organizations suggests that six mailings must be sent to generate one gift (in other words, a donor must be communicated with at least every other month.) Frankly, if your goal is to raise $50,000, then the most effective method would be to pull together your list of lapsed donors (of $1,000 and more) and visit (or call) each one personally. This will help determine which donors could be asked for larger amounts. (Ideally, you want to find one donor who will give $50,000!)

In most organizations, major gifts are solicited personally, and direct mail is used for acquisition and renewal of smaller gifts. Are the one hundred thirty thousand members being solicited regularly? Have you ever done a computerized research screening of this list to determine which members have major gift capacity? That is certainly something to consider. In our experience, in a database of that size there are seventy-five hundred or so major gift prospects you should be soliciting more personally than with direct mail.

In other words, do not worry about how many letters you need to send but contact those lapsed donors as personally (and as soon) as you can, with as much information as you can gather, so that each solicitation has a specific (and appropriate) dollar request.

How can mail be used to move donors to higher levels of giving?

Your database has a number of donors who give $1,000 or more through your direct mail program. It is a general appeal that goes out to your entire database. How do you move the donors to a higher level of giving without taking them out of your direct mail program?

If you have the good fortune of getting gifts of $1,000 or more through the mail, begin personalizing appeals to this group by adding to their letters a thank you for their past gift of $1,000 and a request that they consider a gift this year of $1,500 or whatever amount might be appropriate. We would not take all of these individuals out of the mail program but would add other forms of cultivation: invitations to special events, programs, newsletters with information on how the dollars are spent, and so on.

A next step could be to call and personally thank these donors for their gifts. Then those that respond well to the phone calls could be targeted for face-to-face solicitation. Your message could be "I came to thank you in person for your generosity." Gifts should increase substantially.

These types of activities will move these donors out of the direct mail program and into a major gift program, which might initially affect your ability to meet targets but should increase the total dollars raised at your organization. Before making any decisions, meet with your boss to discuss the possibility of adjusting your targets to include a goal for dollars raised as well as a goal for numbers of major donor prospects identified and cultivated.

How do you manage the multiple goals of increasing average gift size and increasing the donor base, without increasing the budget?

You have just received your goals and budget for the upcoming year. The budget has not changed, but your goals have. You need to increase existing donors' annual giving by 20 percent and double the donor base from 750 to 1,500. Additionally, you are expected to develop a database of 500 potential major donors. To date, you have done nothing more than some acquisition mailings and a few special events.

There are two key problems here. First, fundraising goals should never be developed without significant research on past giving and input from staff, development committee members, and board members. Organizations need to review past giving and then set goals with the involvement of key volunteers (who will help raise the funds by doing face-to-face solicitations).

Second, it is almost impossible to increase both donors and dollar amounts in a year. In fact, in our experience, increasing dollars raised usually happens with fewer donors, not more. Acquisition mailings are expensive and rarely return $1 for the $1 invested. Also, to double your number of donors in a year's time you would actually have to more than double them, because you cannot expect that everyone who gave last year will give again this year. If you need proof of this, review your giving records for the last five years. Have you had 100 percent renewal from donors?

It is tough to tell bosses that their goals are unrealistic. An alternative tack might be to visit with your boss and see if you can determine which is a more important goal: dollars or donors?

What is a good return on second mailings to new donors?

You completed a half-million-piece direct mail campaign to acquire new donors annually. Response rates vary, but they always cover the costs of the mailings. Half of the initial donors from acquisition mailings return with a second gift within twelve months.

This is a good return rate. Some experts suggest that up to ten appeals should be done before you think you have not renewed a donor acquired from an initial acquisition mailing. Having half of them renewing within is year's time is very good. However, you probably need to do a few more mailings before you know exactly how many donors you acquired and how many have renewed.

Is it appropriate to involve board members in a direct mail effort?

If your organization is a very large one with a large budget for direct mail, the answer is probably no. However, if your direct mail efforts are targeted at prospects in your community that might already have a connection to your organization, then your board members and other volunteers can be helpful in a variety of ways.

The first thing they can help do is to build your list. People known to them personally but not to your organization might be much better prospects than names you would buy from a list broker.

Board members can also help you segment and personalize the list as well as serve as letter signers.

We find that it is best not to use board members as actual letter writers or editors. Board members will invariably have their own "expert" opinions on what the letter should say and how it should look. Some might demand one-page letters, no matter how small the type. Others will insist on perfect grammar or business writing, with long paragraphs and long words. Some will cringe at a direct or specific "ask"; and quite often board members will edit out all the emotional appeal of a letter.

When involving board members in list building, letter signing, or anything related to the mail process, it is best to work with volunteers in small groups or one-on-one.

Letters written by a committee tend to be ineffective letters.

Finally, involving your board in your targeted mail campaign is a good way to educate them and introduce them to fundraising in a nonthreatening manner.

Should we sell or lease our mailing list to generate additional revenue?

We know that organizations do sell, trade, or lease their mailing lists. We know that some direct mail experts think that trading lists with other nonprofits is a good way to find acquisition lists that are more profitable. The theory is that if they are giving to another nonprofit, then they are donors and would be more inclined to give to another organization than people who might or might not be donors. We buy the logic that known donors are better prospects than nondonors.

Many list brokers also think this is a good idea. Trading your lists with other nonprofits allows you to get access to other lists for little to no cost, and it gives the list broker one more list to sell, lease, or trade.

In general, however, we are not in favor of this idea, especially if the list comprises your organization's donors, volunteers, sponsors, event participants, and other supporters. In this case, it represents your organization's history and value to the community.

Consider how you got these names in the first place. In almost every case the names you have are probably the result of people trusting your organization with their money (donations) and their personal information (their address, phone number). Do you really want to risk ruining this trust?

It might be hard to remember all the ways in which your list has been built over time. Did a board member at one point make a list of her contacts and suggest that you send them a letter asking for support? How would that board member feel today if she knew you had sold the list and that her friends and associates are being solicited by an organization that is not consistent with her political, spiritual, or cultural beliefs?

Were the sponsors' people that were contacted by years of volunteer committees working on behalf of your organization? Or did you spend hundreds of thousands of dollars over the years to conduct donor acquisition campaigns to find the people in the community who care most about your cause? Will it really be a good return on your acquisition budget to now take this cream of the crop and sell it to someone else who can start soliciting your donors? The governing board should set and approve these decisions, which are matters of institutional policy.

Summary

Many people are looking to direct mail as an immediate solution to some type of fundraising problem. It is simply not an easy way to raise money quickly. Take the long view that it is an excellent way to build a donor base and is initially an investment, much like planned giving, that will pay dividends over time.

CHAPTER SEVEN

SPECIAL EVENTS: MAKING FRIENDS, RAISING FUNDS, AND HAVING FUN

Special events fall into many categories of theme, size, and type of activity. Some are as small as a youth group car wash, and others as large as a gala event that raises millions of dollars. Others include charity golf tournaments, 5K road races and walks, and numerous "a-thons."

These types of activities can help you raise money, strengthen your base of donors and volunteers, clarify your message, and offer your event volunteers an opportunity for immediate and long-term fellowship and fun. However, they can also become all-consuming activities that leave volunteers and staff alike wondering if the results are worth the effort. Or they can become the only source of fundraising for an organization and stunt its ability to engage donors and volunteers in other forms of philanthropic support that lead to larger dollars and long-term support.

No matter what the event's theme, all events require time, effort, and a healthy sense of reality to achieve success. If our e-mail over the past four years is any indication, there are a lot of nonprofits that are looking for a magical, new, creative idea for a special event that produces big revenue with very little work. This imagined magical special event inspires volunteers with its very creativity and easily sells tickets and sponsorships because it is so "unique." No need for hard work and organization. The event just sells itself.

Unfortunately, this type of thinking has been supported somewhat by a few companies and consulting firms who recently have been presenting their products and services as having this same kind of effect. "Your board does not have to ask for money," their sales literature promises. "Just fill the tables with people, and they will give," others say. "Put our shopping mall on your website, and you will start receiving money with little effort in no time," some dot-com companies promised.

This chapter will help you apply sound fundraising principles to special events to increase their impact. The principles of "flooring" the campaign, strong volunteer leadership, and sequential fund raising apply to special events just as much as they do to annual and capital campaigns. This chapter covers answers to the following questions:

- How do I prepare to have a successful fundraising event?
- Where can I find special event ideas or themes?
- We will be selling tickets to our upcoming event. What other kinds of revenue opportunities should we consider for our special event?
- What role do sponsors play in an event?
- What is the best approach to securing an event sponsor?
- What are some ways to recognize event sponsors?
- What is the best way to sell tickets to an event—in blocks or individually?
- What can we do not only to sell tickets but also to fill seats?
- Should we allow outside vendors to hold events for our benefit?
- What is the appropriate way to determine tax-deductible credit for event participants?
- Should event sponsors be recognized in our annual gift clubs?
- How do you create special events that contribute to a healthy, sustainable development program?
- How many events should an organization conduct each year?

How do I prepare to have a successful fundraising event?

First, understand the role that volunteer leadership needs to play in the success of your event and seek ways to involve the very best volunteers you can. The event chairperson should be someone who can recruit a lot of people to help in the event, solicit significant sponsorship dollars, and work hard to make the event a success. First-time events need a working chairperson, not just honorary people who lend their names. Spend as much time as you need to identify and recruit the right chairperson.

To prepare for the recruitment, it is a good idea to write an initial draft of the plan for your event, as well as a job description for the event leaders. It does not have to be elaborate, but it does need to show volunteers the keys to the event's success. For examples of a job description and a simple event plan, see Exhibits 7.1 and 7.2.

EXHIBIT 7.1.   SPECIAL EVENT CHAIRPERSON JOB DESCRIPTION.

The event chairperson is the leader of this effort. The chairperson sets the pace and tone for the event and supports the volunteer solicitors in their efforts. The chairperson is actively involved in conceptualizing the event, planning logistics, recruiting volunteers, and soliciting underwriters and sponsors. The candidates who will be considered for the position are respected by the board and the organization, have access to corporate and individual resources in the community, and are able to recruit and lead a strong group of organized volunteers. Specifically, the chairperson will perform the following tasks:

- Work closely with the director of development to set goals for the event and ensure those goals are met
- Oversee the event timetable
- Recruit chairs for each needed subcommittee (subcommittees might include corporate sponsors, patrons and benefactors, logistics, entertainment and publicity, ticket sales, accounting, and so on)
- Hold regular meetings of the subcommittee chairs
- Actively participate in the solicitation of key event underwriters and sponsors
- Attend the event and serve as a key host and spokesperson
- Thank sponsors, underwriters, and other participants
- Participate in postevent evaluation and help secure next year's chairperson

Before choosing to do a special event and picking one that is right for your organization, it is wise to run a quick readiness assessment by asking yourself the following questions:

- Do you have good potential to recruit an event chairperson or co-chairs? A planning committee? A treasurer? A volunteer coordinator?
- Are your leaders also people who can make things happen, through the resources they have? Do they have access to corporate funding or sponsorships?
- Do you have experienced leadership or input from experienced event producers at your disposal, whether they are consultants or volunteers?
- What type of event would appeal most to your audience or your consumers? The popular one your community has supported in the past or a new and exciting one?
- How much money do you need to raise, without fail?
- What are your costs (the projected expenses) to put on the event? How many of these could you get donated as gifts in kind? Do you want or need to use corporate sponsorships? How will you do this? Who will make the calls?
- How many volunteers can you realistically count on to plan the event? To stage the event?

EXHIBIT 7.2. SPECIAL EVENT PLAN SAMPLE.

Valentine's Day Concert

Goal: $40,000 (net)

The Valentine's Day Concert will raise funds to support [name of organization's] scholarship fund for low-income children. Success of this event will hinge upon the early commitment of three large underwriters. Their willingness to finance a large portion of the event's expenses will contribute to the event's appeal and the community perception of the worthiness of the concert's beneficiary, our organization.

The [historic hall] downtown has been secured to host the concert and [big name entertainer] has been confirmed.

The following outlines key activities for the concert committee and staff:

1. Recruit the concert chair by March 1.
2. By May 1, with chair's assistance, enlist five to ten people (sponsors and ticket committee) from outside the board of directors to assist in selling sponsorships, friends' tickets, and tickets.
3. Develop list of potential underwriters and prepare sponsorship packets by May 1.
4. With concert chair's assistance, solicit event underwriters by September 1.
5. Send list of potential sponsors to the board of directors and the sponsor and ticket committee on September 30.
6. Assign all sponsor prospects by October 15.
7. Complete sponsor solicitation by December 1.
8. Begin general ticket sales on January 15.
9. Host event.
10. Send thank you notes to event underwriters and sponsors.

- Have you allowed enough time to plan and execute all tasks? In our experience, new events should be given at least twelve months to plan, if not more.
- What other expectations for this event do you have in addition to raising money? Have you taken steps to appoint a committee chair for each one of these areas? If building the strength of your board is an expectation, will all board members be actively involved? If getting your mission and message out to the community is an expectation, do you have a publicity plan?
- Are you prepared to communicate to all workers what you expect of them? This will create enthusiasm and help them take initiative. Have you considered how you will thank and recognize volunteers?

- Have you considered all facets of what to expect in terms of time, expenses, and unforeseen difficulties?
- What kind of experience will the event guests and participants have? After you have done an agenda for the event, take an objective view of it and think in terms of what a guest and a participant will experience at every moment. Will they have positive experiences from beginning to end? Be sure to consider the following details:

>   City permits
>   Insurance
>   Lighting
>   Liquor license
>   Parking and transportation
>   Receipt books for items sold or auctioned
>   Restrooms
>   Sound and visibility of program
>   Temperature
>   Weather conditions
>   Wheelchair access

Where can I find special event ideas or themes?

We have included a partial list of ideas in Exhibit 7.3. While this is a good starting point, in the long run you might want to consider event ideas that can become signature events that are closely associated with your organization and that fit well with your mission.

We will be selling tickets to our upcoming event. What other kinds of revenue opportunities should we consider for our special event?

You can create opportunities for underwriters, sponsors, table sponsors, raffles, auction items, sales of items such as T-shirts, and so on. Your event invitation can also offer people the opportunity to make a donation above and beyond the ticket price or in lieu of buying tickets.

What role do sponsors play in an event?

Sponsors generally pay a premium to connect their brand to your event. Most events have different levels of sponsorships with various types of benefits for each level. A very large sponsor that is paying and giving more than any other sponsor might be called a *signature sponsor* or an *underwriter*. What should that cost? It

EXHIBIT 7.3. SPECIAL EVENT IDEAS AND THEMES.

Auctions

- Art
- Furniture
- Silent auction

Balls or Dances

- Charity balls
- Square dances

Concerts

- Country music with square dancing
- Jazz
- Rock
- Single recording artists
- Well-known singers mixed with local groups
- Youth singers or bands

Craft Shows and Sales

- Dolls
- Jewelry, especially ethnic
- Kitchen items
- Linens
- Pottery
- Quilts
- Silverware
- "Survival kits" for camp or exams
- Bake sale
- Candy sale
- Flower/plant sale
- Tag sale

Contests or Drawings

- Baby picture contest
- Basketball free-throw contest
- Dessert or chili cook-off
- Entertainment book drawing
- Gift basket contest
- Halloween costume contest
- Miniature golf putting contest
- Penny wars
- Pie-eating/throwing contest
- Prom photo contest

(Continued)

EXHIBIT 7.3.   Continued.

Dinners

- Celebrity waiter or waitress
- Dinner and auction
- Celebrity speaker
- Casino night
- House party

Endurance or Fitness Pledge Events

- Biathlons
- Dance-a-thons
- Marathons
- "Rock-a-thons"
- Triathlons
- Walks

Exhibitions, Displays, or Shows

- Art exhibitions
- Fashion shows
- Flower shows

Fairs or Festivals

- Country or state fairs: food, crafts, and contests
- International fairs: food, crafts, and art

Food Events

- Bake-off contests
- Barbeques
- Box lunches or dinners for shut-ins
- Catered food delivered to ill patients at home or to mothers of newborn babies
- House parties
- Open houses
- Picnics
- Spaghetti dinners on the night before local sporting event, like a road race
- Booths at sporting events or antique or crafts sales

Fun Runs and Walks (Especially Health-Related Causes or School or Club Programs)

- 5K
- 10K

Holiday, Ethnic, and International Themes

- Christmas
- Halloween: hayrides, haunted house tours, or gym booths
- Hanukkah
- New Year's
- Valentine's Day
- Country fairs
- Mardi Gras or "Carnival"
- Oktoberfest
- Winter carnivals
- Food or art from around the world, in a fair format

Merchandise Sales

- Attic sales
- Bake sales
- Crafts, of all kinds and in all locales
- Estate sales
- Food booths: popcorn, cotton candy, hot dogs, pizza, snow cones, ice cream
- Garage sales
- Plant sales
- Herb garden sales
- Rummage sales

Ticket Events

- Art exhibits
- Bazaars
- Bingo
- Celebrity or distinguished speakers
- Concerts
- Fairs
- Festivals
- Flower shows
- Talent shows
- Theater

Tournament Events (Give Donation to Play)

- Fishing
- Golf
- Tennis

Tours (Single Location or Multiple)

- Decorators' "showhouse"
- "Expeditions": grand-scale outdoor events (such as mountain climbing or canoeing)
- Garden

might be more than the costs of the event, but sponsorships should at least cover the costs of the event.

What is the best approach to securing an event sponsor?

Just like other forms of fundraising, sharing a strong case for support during a personal, face-to-face solicitation is the most effective method for securing sponsorships. By meeting with a prospective sponsor, you can better understand the goals they have and carefully tailor your sponsorship proposal to meet their needs. For example, if a potential sponsor tells you that giving their executives an opportunity to meet with the event participants is important, be sure that your sponsorship benefits package includes VIP tickets to the event.

It is a good idea to have a letter or proposal to request sponsorships, and these are best hand-delivered at a meeting or sent after a face-to-face meeting. Letters can never convey the excitement a volunteer has about your event or the passion you have for your organization; nor can letters help you find the sponsorship packages that best suit your prospects' goals and objectives.

With this in mind, Exhibit 7.4 presents a sample letter that assumes a meeting has been held.

What are some ways to recognize event sponsors?

We can remember days when companies sponsored events because the CEO or other corporate officer liked the benefiting organization and wanted to support it. In fact, one of Kristina's most successful special events was a bowl-a-thon that received more than $25,000 in corporate sponsorships, even though the costs of the event were less than $1,000. The bowl-a-thon did not have a high profile or a lot of media exposure. The only recognition the sponsors received was an imprint of their logo on the event T-shirts. However, the CEO of a local bank was involved with the organization and convinced two other banks to match his bank's sponsorship.

These days, more and more corporations have to prove that every dollar they spend will help the company's stock price or sales. So when it comes to attracting and maintaining event sponsors, stewardship is one of the most important fundraising principles to keep in mind. Providing data to sponsors on the impact of their dollars is essential to maintaining sponsors, especially corporate sponsors, in this highly competitive marketplace.

With this in mind, we offer you the three most important ways to recognize event sponsors:

EXHIBIT 7.4.   SPECIAL EVENT SPONSOR SOLICITATION LETTER.

Name of Decision Maker
Title
Name of Company
Street Address
City, State Zip

Dear [decision maker],

Thank you for meeting with [other person's name] and me last Tuesday. We appreciate your commitment to considering a title sponsorship ($40,000) of our upcoming dinner and silent auction benefiting our new ABC Program. As a title sponsor, your company will receive the following:

- Lead listing in all event promotions, including [names]
- A premier table seating eight at the dinner and silent auction
- A listing on our event website, www.[organization name here].org

    Based upon our estimates, your company name and logo will be seen by 55,000 people as a result of your sponsorship. Last year's event drew more than 250 business owners and executives from the local community. We are anticipating an even larger audience this year.

    As you know, the dinner and silent auction will benefit our ABC Program. When we reach our goal for the event of raising $250,000, ABC Program will be able to help 1,200 more children learn the value of reading.

    Thank you once again for considering our request. Please let me know if you need any additional information. Otherwise, I will call you on Thursday to further discuss this opportunity with you and to learn of your decision.

Best Regards,

[name]

Event Chairperson

P.S.: I am pleased to report that WABC has agreed to be our media sponsor. This will create even more positive exposure for our title sponsor.

1. Tell them up front and in writing what they will get for their sponsorship. Refer to Exhibit 7.4. Be sure to include information on the following:
   - Where will their logo be seen?
   - How many people will hear about their company or see their logo as a result of the sponsorship?
   - What is the audience for the event? Does this market fit with the company's market?
   - How many other sponsors will be allowed to participate at the same levels or higher?

2. Deliver on your promises. Make sure that your sponsors get all the benefits you told them they would. Making sponsors happy takes attention to detail. For example, if you tell them their logo will be on a banner draped across your parade float, make sure it is. Although it was more than ten years ago, Kristina will never forget how awful it felt to see her organization's float glide through a St. Patrick's Day parade without the sponsor's banner. The sponsor had delivered it on time, but it was neatly rolled up on the floor of the float storage garage. The volunteers assembling the float did not know what it was, so they left it in the garage.

3. Prior to the event and especially after the event, report to your sponsors, both verbally and in writing, with the results of the event and their sponsorship. By providing them with data on the impact of their sponsorship dollars, you will help them show the bottom-line results of this and future sponsorships. And because so few organizations do this, let alone do this well, you will gain a competitive advantage over other sponsor seekers. This report should mirror your original proposal.

Here are some creative ways to recognize sponsors:

- Create a listing on your website.
- List them on all event promotional materials, including invitations.
- Provide them with special seating, tickets, and so on.
- Include sponsor logos and company names in all event advertisements, PSAs, and so on.
- Put sponsor logos on billboards that promote the event.
- Provide special participation programs for employees, such as framing a house.
- Seek to co-brand materials. (*Co-branding* is a way the company also promotes its involvement through its own marketing materials, products, and services.)
- Be sure to have signage and other visibility at the event.
- Imprint their logo on door prizes.

- Print a thank you letter in the newspaper.
- Print a thank you letter and distribute it to the corporation's employees.
- Consider banners, flags, bumper stickers, posters, and stickers with corporate logos that volunteers and others can wear at the event, put on mailing envelopes, and so on.
- For smaller companies, consider bringing employees bagels and coffee when you preannounce the event.
- For larger companies, work with the human resources department to create special community involvement programs.
- Create volunteer opportunities for their employees at the event.

What is the best way to sell tickets to an event—in blocks or individually?

A brand new social service organization contacted us because they were planning their first benefit gala. The gala facility could hold three hundred people, and they wanted to charge $100 per ticket with a goal of earning $30,000. They were not sure how they should approach selling three hundred tickets. Did they need thirty volunteers to sell ten tickets each? Or was there another formula they could follow?

We shared with them that most special events rely on some type of volunteer structure to help sell tickets and some kind of table sponsorships to sell blocks of tickets. In other words, by recruiting as many volunteers as possible, you can increase your likelihood of selling more tickets and of having people actually attend the event.

In the case of three hundred tickets, we would recruit an event chairperson (or perhaps a ticket or sponsor chairperson who reports to the event chairperson) and ask him to recruit three to five excellent volunteers to buy and sell 40 percent of the tickets in blocks of eight to create table sponsors. We might consider making the table sponsorship cost $1,000 and giving each table sponsor eight tickets along with a listing in a program book. The key to this part of the strategy is making sure the volunteers who are selling table sponsorships are first table sponsors themselves.

The chairperson would then recruit six or seven volunteers to buy and sell an additional 40 percent of the tickets in blocks of four and call these *partial-table* or *joint-table sponsors* (priced at $500).

Finally, the event chairperson would recruit as many volunteers as possible to focus on selling the remaining 20 percent of tickets at the $100 price.

In our experience, to sell more tickets you need more volunteers who will commit to both buying and selling tickets. It is not as much fun to look at empty seats and tables.

What can we do not to only sell the tickets but also to fill seats?

As people have become more and more pressed for time, this has become a challenge for many organizations—and it can create a poor reputation for your event.
Which would you rather attend, an event for which you have to buy your tickets
a year in advance, or one that always has plenty of empty seats? Most people
would rather attend an event that has too many people and not enough chairs.
It is exciting and adds prestige to the event.

If people are buying tickets but not attending, it could mean a few things.
First, your supporters might be ready to just send in their checks instead of buy
tickets. Review your past events and determine who buys tickets and does not
attend. Next year, ask these people to support the annual fund instead of the event.

Second, your volunteers might not be doing enough to promote attendance.
We have a good friend in Atlanta who has served as a volunteer chairperson for
many events. According to her, the secret to getting people to the event is calling
each of them, verbally confirming their attendance, and making them aware of
who else is attending. It might be a lot to ask an event chair or event volunteers to
call everyone who buys a ticket and confirm all attendees, but it works. Our friend
reports that she has rarely had an empty chair at one of her events.

If you find people who are not going to use their tickets, ask them to return
the tickets and then make sure you do not set a table for them. Just be sure to list
them in the program book and send them a copy.

Should we allow outside vendors to hold events for our benefit?

Unless the event management company or vendor is a 501(c)(3) organization,
the donors cannot claim any deduction for contributions they give directly to the
vendor.

Before you consider whether or not you will allow an outside vendor to host
an event in your honor, it is best to develop a policy on the matter. The policy
should be discussed with your development committee and then presented to
the board for approval. The policy should address the following questions:

- What is the total amount of money the group should raise? If the group thinks
  it will only raise $500, should the event still be held?
- How much of your organization's staff time and resources can be put into
  the event? Will you only work with other groups that do everything themselves?
- Will you provide the vendor with lists of names of your donors and volunteers?
  Or will you only work with companies that can bring in new supporters?

- How much do you want a group to spend relative to how much you will receive? If a group spends $100,000 to raise money in your name, pays its staff $50,000, has other expenses totaling $35,000, and sends you $15,000, will you be happy? If not, you might want to have a statement in your policy that says that you will only work with groups that expect to have net revenues equal to a certain percentage of total dollars raised.
- How will the group verify dollars raised versus expenses? Do they have systems in place for this?
- How much interaction with event ticket buyers, participants, and so on will you have? Will you receive a list of the people who buy tickets to the event with their addresses? Or are you happy just to get the money? (We tend to like to know who attended and have the opportunity to follow up with them.)
- If the group offering to do the event has had bad public relations or financial scandals in the last year, will you still let them do an event for you?

The policies need to reflect your organization's mission, beliefs, and ethics, and sometimes it is hard to discuss these types of things if you already have a vendor promising to raise thousands of dollars for you. So try to have your policy in place before you already know what someone is offering.

What is the appropriate way to determine tax-deductible credit for event participants?

As of the writing of this book, in the United States, the IRS requires nonprofit organizations to tell donors whether or not they have received any goods or services for a donation of $75 or more. And the value of these goods and services reduces the amount of the contribution that is eligible for a deduction. So when planning a special event, it is a good idea to recruit an accountant to the event committee and ask him or her to help establish the tax-deductible portion of each participant's fee. This gives you a great way to involve one more person in your event. In the case of a golf tournament, for example, where a foursome is paying $1,400 to play golf, the tax-deductible portion will be that amount that is left from the participants' fees after you subtract some fair market value for green fees, cart rental, any food and drink that is provided, and any entertainment that has a market value. In other words, if it would usually cost a foursome $300 to play at your golf course, plus $50 for the carts, and they are getting $200 worth of food and drinks, then the tax-deductible portion would be $1,400 minus $550, which is $850.

When it comes to auctions, following the rules sometimes gets tricky. For example, if someone gives you an antique chair and says it is worth $400, but you sell it at the auction for $600, do they get a tax deduction for $400 or $600? Here's why this is tricky: the contributor of the chair is responsible for establishing its fair market value, and if he wants to use the sales price as the fair market value, then he might say that its fair market value was $600. However, if he does this, the person who bought the chair has no charitable deduction because she paid $600 for a $600 chair.

If the donor of the chair establishes that it is worth $400, and the person who buys it pays $600, then the person might have made a $200 charitable contribution. We say *might have made* because it is the purchaser's responsibility to establish that a charitable contribution was made.

In either case, you should receipt the transaction as a purchase of goods. If the purchaser can substantiate that she paid in excess of the fair market value, then she is entitled to a tax deduction for the excess. Again, this is her responsibility. You can facilitate this exchange of information but should not make any claims regarding the fair market value; merely report what the chair donor told you.

You can write a letter to the chair buyer that thanks her for attending the auction and buying the chair. In the letter, you can list the price paid for the chair and include a full description of it. Then include a statement of the donor's established fair market value. For example, you could write, "When the chair was given to us for the auction, we were told that it had a fair market value of $400. You will need to verify this for your tax records. The auction raised more than [dollar amount]."

Fortunately, we have found that the IRS's website, www.irs.gov, is quite user friendly and holds a host of information that you might find helpful in these kinds of circumstances. For example, Publication 4221, *Compliance Guide for 501(c)(3) Tax-Exempt Organizations,* explains the record keeping, report filing, and disclosure rules that apply to organizations that have tax-exempt status under section 501(c)(3). It can be found at the following link: www.irs.gov/pub/irs-pdf/p4221.pdf.

IRS Publication 1771, *Charitable Contributions Substantiation and Disclosure Requirements,* is one that every development office should have. It can be found at www.irs.gov/pub/irs-pdf/p1771.pdf.

And finally, IRS Publication 561, *Determining the Value of Donated Property,* is a good one to share with donors of noncash items. It can be found at www.irs.gov/pub/irs-pdf/p561.pdf.

Should event sponsors be recognized in our annual gift clubs?

Generally, no. You should recognize event sponsors as event sponsors and create specific ways of recognizing them that relates to the event. Event sponsor recognition should be kept separate from annual giving level recognition. Why? Because when a company sponsors an event, some of its money is going toward expenses related to recognizing it, as well expenses of the event. And the company is generally receiving some kind of benefit (such as tickets to the event or advertising) for making its sponsorship. On the other hand, someone giving to the annual campaign typically is giving to general unrestricted funds and receiving little, if any, benefit for his or her gift.

Gifts made for unrestricted purposes are some of the most valuable dollars a nonprofit can receive. Donors who make these types of gifts deserve special recognition.

How do you create special events that contribute to a healthy, sustainable development program?

First, recognize that conducting special events is not a one-size-fits-all proposition. Events and strategies for larger, more mature organizations can differ significantly from those for smaller, newer nonprofits.

Second, recognize that events are an excellent way to make potential donors aware of your organization's mission but should not be the only manner in which you ask for support.

Third, look for ways to use events to involve new volunteers in your fundraising efforts and not just burn out your usual supporters. Remember, it is often easier to introduce volunteers to the art of asking by getting them involved in selling tickets to an event before involving them in asking for philanthropic donations. But once they are skilled in their art of asking, it is time to give them new challenges in your overall development program.

Fourth, use highly publicized and well-conducted events to build name recognition for your organization and provide precious unrestricted funds.

Fifth, carefully evaluate the impact of each event that you do. Review the net amount raised versus resources spent, the number of new volunteers who participated, the number of new "friends" acquired for your organization, and other ancillary benefits. Both small and larger organizations have one thing in common: for those that have many annual special events, analyses will help to determine if it is best to focus on one or a few rather than many. If you take the approach that fewer events are better you will generally receive more net revenue dollars, and staff and volunteer burnout is less likely to occur.

Sixth, do not just copy what someone else is doing. Special events need to be studied carefully, not just copied from other experiences. Find an event that is right for your organization, resources, image, and support levels from your local community.

Finally, remember that, like other fundraising initiatives such as direct mail and planned giving, it takes time to produce high profitability from newly conceived events. We find that many mega-events take seven or more years to reach the level of annually producing seven-figure revenues.

How many events should an organization conduct each year?

We have found no magic number of events an organization should conduct. For example, Kristina worked with one organization that had five events a year: a gala, a 5K road race, a concert, an entry in a parade float contest, and a walk-a-thon. It was a new organization trying to raise money for programs that helped people with mental illness lead productive lives. The events were great because they created community awareness about the programs. However, they really took a toll on the board, the volunteers, and Kristina's big staff of two.

In retrospect, Kristina would say this was a classic example of an organization that had "special-eventitis": the tendency to think that the only way to raise money or increase donations is to have more events. "Special-eventitis" also expresses itself through one or more of the following traits:

- Any time there is a budget shortfall, board members start talking about a great golf tournament they attended or other event ideas.
- Board members are starting to use terms such as *burn out* and *new blood*.
- Staff is tired of picking napkin colors and discussing seating charts.
- Total fundraising costs consistently exceed 40 percent of all dollars raised.
- Event revenue is stagnant or decreasing.
- Sponsors are complaining about the number of solicitations they are receiving from an organization.
- The community knows your organization's events better than it knows your programs and mission.
- The same volunteers are involved with every event.
- Board members are reluctant to approve new programs because it will require having another event to raise the money.

What's the cure for "special-eventitis"? The simple answer is to go out and ask people to make contributions to support your mission and programs. The more professional answer is to start an annual fund campaign. For more thoughts on starting or improving an annual fund, see Chapter Five.

Summary

Conduct your events using sound fundraising campaign principles. Recruit and involve as much volunteer leadership as possible. Create a theme for your event and incorporate it in all aspects of the event. Always have a dual purpose for events: raising funds and identifying additional people to further involve in your mission. In order to raise significantly more money, take the identification of special event donors to the next level by seeking their additional support for your organization through more personal solicitations unrelated to the event. For example, try to make sure all special event attendees are regularly solicited for annual giving. This approach can more fully justify the time and effort put into conducting a special event.

CHAPTER EIGHT

MAJOR GIFTS: GETTING TO THE BIG GIFTS

Each year the *Chronicle of Philanthropy* releases a study called the Philanthropy 400. The 2004 study showed that of the $240.72 billion given to nonprofits in 2003, 20 percent went to 400 organizations, suggesting that $1 out of every $5 raised went to only 400 nonprofits. Left were nearly one million other nonprofits to split the remaining 80 percent. The Philanthropy 400 study also showed that as of 2003 there continued to be a trend in which fewer donors provided most of the contributions to many big organizations. Therefore, this trend is changing the ways in which these top 400 fundraise.

Some of these top 400 organizations reported that they were investing significant resources to pursue major gifts and are beginning to move away from other traditional fundraising methods such as broad-based mailing solicitation and special events. Instead, these larger nonprofits are spending more money to hire major gift and planned giving officers and are devoting major resources to attempt to educate donors on various ways to give (Hall and others, 2004).

Because a major gifts program can be the way to raise large dollars quickly at a very low cost, a successful major gifts program is the eventual goal of virtually every nonprofit organization. Sounds like fundraising heaven, doesn't it? It can be, but major gift success does not come easily or quickly. It is based on successfully engaging donors in your organization over time.

Regardless of their wealth, most donors do not make their first gift to you a major gift. In other words, there are not very many (if any) rich strangers who find your organization on their own to give you money.

Major gifts usually come from people who are current or former board members, long-time donors, or community leaders who believe strongly in your mission.

Major gifts are the result of continual personal interactions between donors and your organization. A fancy brochure or proposal presented to a rich person (who has no previous connection to your organization) will rarely result in a major gift. If you are explaining your mission during the solicitation, it is not time to ask for a major gift.

The secret is to match your opportunities with donor's philanthropic interests. Your personal involvement with that donor enables you to understand the donor's needs and create a win-win fundraising situation. As you saw in the Hierarchy of Fundraising (Figure 2.1), major gifts should begin after a mature annual fund program is developed or as the next phase of fundraising after a capital campaign.

In this chapter, we answer the following questions:

- What gift level is considered a major gift?
- We are a small organization. How do we start a major gift program?
- What role should volunteers and board members have in our major gift program?
- How should I prepare our volunteers for participation in a major gift solicitation?
- How do I market the case for unrestricted major gifts?
- Should I measure the results of a major gifts officer purely by dollars raised, or by some other figure?
- What are call reports and why are they used?
- I am trying to revamp our major gift clubs. Should I offer premiums?
- How do I handle mailing deadlines that conflict with the holidays?
- Is it a good idea to have group dinners, lunches, and other such events as a way to cultivate major donors?
- How can I sell a major donor on the idea of giving enough to rename our facility in his honor?

What gift level is considered a major gift?

The level of a major gift is different for every organization. To determine which one is for your organization, prepare a Range of Gifts Table (see Tables 2.1 through 2.4) to show the gift sizes you need at various levels. Typically the top fifty to one hundred gifts (in size) that you need are major gifts that should be solicited face-to-face. For some organizations, $1,000 is considered a major annual gift. For others a major gift could be $10,000 or more.

We are a small organization. How do we start a major gift program?

As part of your organization's strategic planning process, begin to identify a new project or endowment that would interest a major donor. Then get your best two fundraising board members to go over your current list of individual donors. Try to identify fifteen to twenty individuals who already provide financial support to your organization, who have seldom or never been contacted personally, and who might have significant financial resources.

If your list of current donors is rather large (more than a couple thousand) you might want to conduct an electronic database screening with a company such as MaGIC. They research your entire list, identify wealthy and philanthropic people, and then help you develop a plan for contacting the people identified.

Once you have your short list, make a plan for visiting each individual on your list. It helps if someone on your board knows each individual and can arrange meetings. You should plan to visit each individual one at a time. Have your talking points ready to share with them. Tell them about the goals of your organization, how many people you hope to reach in the coming years, and how they and philanthropic giving can make a difference.

If you do not currently have gift clubs, you might want to establish giving levels for your major gift program. Ultimately, you want your board focusing its fundraising efforts on personal solicitation of major gifts and your volunteer fundraising committee coordinating special events and other such projects.

What role should volunteers and board members have in our major gift program?

Ideally, your board members will all be involved in your major gift program in one or more of the following ways:

1. Helping to identify major gift prospects
2. Cultivating major gift prospects by inviting them to events, tours, and meetings at your organization
3. Soliciting major gift prospects
4. Ensuring that major gifts are spent as the donor intended
5. Being major gift donors themselves (this is the most important of all)

As peer-to-peer solicitation is the most effective and efficient form of fundraising, your major gifts program should involve the recruitment and training of volunteers who also assist in the solicitation of major gifts. The job description for a major gifts chairperson (in Exhibit 8.1) outlines the key major gift activities for volunteers.

How should I prepare our volunteers for participation in a major gift solicitation?

If you have volunteers who get all excited about the major gifts program but then get "cold feet" when they have to do the solicitations, do not be surprised. The fear of failure can be very powerful. At first, most people say they do not enjoy fundraising. Therefore you need to find ways to build their confidence.

You can do this by providing them with a strategy memo that clearly shows that the prospect has the capacity to give a major gift, has an interest in your organization, and has a history of giving gifts at the level you are requesting. While it is not feasible to create a strategy memo for each and every solicitation your organization conducts, it is worthwhile to make it a practice for your major donor solicitations. Exhibit 8.2 provides a sample strategy memo.

EXHIBIT 8.1.   MAJOR GIFTS CHAIRPERSON JOB DESCRIPTION.

The chair of the major gifts subcommittee is responsible to the chair of the board development committee for overseeing [name of organization's] major gifts program.

Specifically, that involves leading the subcommittee in the following areas:

- Recruiting three to five persons capable of credibly identifying, cultivating, and soliciting prospective donors in the [dollar amount] range.
- Participating in the identification of annual, capital, and endowment projects appropriate for major gift solicitation.
- Reviewing and approving [organization's] annual major gifts plan.
- Developing recommendations to the development committee on named gift opportunities for both facilities and endowment funds.
- Developing recommendations to the development committee on other recognition activities.
- Reviewing [organization's] stewardship program to ensure adequate response to major gift donors.
- Making a personal major gift.
- Annually personally soliciting three to five persons for major gifts.

EXHIBIT 8.2.   STRATEGY MEMO.

CONFIDENTIAL
[name of organization]
Strategy Memo
prepared for
[solicitor's name]

Board Member: Jane Smith

Address: Mr. and Mrs. J. John Smith (Jane)

3455 Wood Road, NW

Dalton, Georgia 30399

(404) 123-4567

(404) 123-7890 fax

Evaluation: $100,000 over five years

Our Organization Giving History:

2002	$10,000	Annual campaign
	$2,500	Our event table sponsor
2001	$5,000	Annual campaign
	$200	Event ticket
2000	$5,000	Annual campaign
	$2,500	Our event table sponsor
1999	$2,500	Our event table sponsor
1998	$1,000	Annual campaign
1997	$1,000	Annual campaign
1996	$500	Annual campaign
1995	$500	Annual campaign
1994	$500	Annual campaign
TOTAL	$31,200	

Background Information

- Jane is one of our largest donors.
- Jane is a new member of the board of trustees.
- The Smiths were instrumental in securing a $20,000 challenge grant for the 2002 annual campaign from the B. T. Smith Foundation. In the past, the foundation has not given to our organization.
- Jane is also the current president for the City Arts Foundation. Under her leadership, City Arts is supporting the Impressionist Show in 2001.

- Jane serves on the boards of the Community Outreach Mission, the Education Board, the University of [State], and the private local school.
- The Smiths give $10,000 per year to the United Way and give regularly to several other charities at a level ranging from $1,000 to $15,000.

Other Information

Jane's husband, John Smith, was born in 1940 in Memphis. He received his undergraduate degree from Princeton University in 1962 and his graduate degree in business administration from Harvard in 1964. He is chair of [company name 1] and directly and indirectly owns 1,153,954 shares as of 8/26/99, valued at $22 million (as of 12/28/04). He owns 40,881 shares of [company name 2] as of 3/1/04, valued at $1 million (as of 12/28/04). He owns 9,000 shares of [company name 3] (as of 4/5/04) valued at $135,000 (as of 12/28/04).

Mr. Smith serves on several corporate boards:

- Ford Motor Credit Company
- Crawfish & Company
- ABC Corporation
- Carpet Industries
- Big Banks of Georgia

Mr. Smith serves on two foundation boards:

- B. T. Smith Foundation
- ABC Foundation

Strategy

Set a meeting with Jane at her home or another place that is convenient for her. Ask if she would like John to meet with the two of you. During the meeting, outline the need for the project and the opportunities it will create for the organization. Then ask them to consider a major gift of $100,000 (payable over a period of up to five years) for the new program scholarships. This gift would be above and beyond regular annual giving.

Talking Points

- Thank you for your ongoing financial support of our organization and for your service on the board. You have been very generous to our organization.
- We especially appreciate your help in getting the challenge grant from the B. T. Smith Foundation.
- As you know, our organization is in the early stages of setting up a new program and will utilize scholarship support to enable young people to participate. [Explain the program and answer questions as needed.]

(Continued)

EXHIBIT 8.2.   Continued.

- This is an exciting time for us, and in order to reach our goal of serving fifty new people in this program, it will be imperative for each board member to give at the highest level possible.
- To date, three board members have made gifts totaling $350,000, with a lead gift of $250,000 from Bob and Betty Bradford. So we're off to a great start.
- As you know, it will be crucial to have 100 percent participation from the board. This is extremely important when we visit foundations and corporations, so the board is the first group we are soliciting in the campaign. We must prove to the rest of the philanthropic leaders in Dalton that we are behind the work of our organization. And we must set a standard of giving for others.
- This is a big project, and it needs big commitments. The funds we raise from within our membership will set the tone for the rest of our efforts.
- I am here today to ask you for a commitment to the campaign. On behalf of the board of trustees, I hope you will consider a pledge of $100,000 to support scholarships for our new program. Pledges can be paid over a five-year period and are in addition to regular annual giving and membership.
- Most importantly, once you have asked them to consider the pledge, make them respond without your interruption.

[Answer questions and determine when you can follow up.]

Reviewing the strategy memo with volunteers prior to the solicitations also affords you the opportunity to discuss who will have the responsibility for actually making the "ask" in the meeting. As you assign prospects for solicitations, try to make each volunteer's first call be on a prospect who you think will be most likely to say yes to the request.

How do I market the case for unrestricted major gifts?

Your school just recently completed a capital campaign. Now you want to begin an ongoing major gifts program. The board of trustees has not yet finalized future bricks-and-mortar needs. So you will be asking donors to consider supporting endowment needs.

Take a thorough look at your budget to see if there are other items that would interest a donor: faculty development, travel, athletic equipment, library books, computer needs, science lab equipment, and so on.

For larger major gifts, you can consider endowing and naming some of these types of items, such as the Joe Smith Faculty Development Fund.

There are two other strategies that you might want to consider: (1) establishing annual giving clubs at levels much higher than you already have and asking donors to join the higher club level; and (2) establishing cumulative giving societies, which can increase individuals' lifetime giving. Challenge gifts are also an excellent way to secure major gifts. Ask a donor to give a gift to match all new gifts from grandparents or new parents as a way to secure a major gift and new donors at the same time.

When starting a major gift program after a capital campaign it is also good to do a thorough analysis of your campaign donors and look for those who underdonated significantly as a way to build your prospect pool. Usually these are donors that you thought could give $250,000 but gave $25,000 (or similar amounts). These donors might be good major gifts donors, with more cultivation.

Should I measure the results of a major gifts officer purely by dollars raised, or by some other figure?

You have a major gifts officer reporting to you who is telecommuting from his home in Philadelphia. How should you measure his results from your office in Cleveland?

In our experience, a development professional whose sole job is major gifts should be able to have up to 150 major donors or prospects that will be seen in a twelve-month period.

Of these 150, 30 percent should be for first calls to qualify the prospect as a potential major donor, 25 percent should be ready to move toward a solicitation, 25 percent should be solicitations, and 20 percent should be for stewardship.

Of course, 150 is not manageable if the development officer has other duties. To establish a reasonable number, use 150 and multiply by the total amount of time the staff person is to spend on major gifts. For example, if the staff person is to spend 50 percent of his time on major gifts and 50 percent on other duties, then the number of prospects they manage should be close to seventy-five.

To monitor this person's activity, it is essential to have the major gift officer prepare weekly call reports showing whom he contacted and the results of each contact. The weekly call reports should also list whom he intends to contact next week. The production of call reports can be made easier with various kinds of software programs. In fact, some commercially available fundraising software programs now integrate with Microsoft Outlook and other contact management tools that are good for tracking which prospects have been seen, what the results of the contact were, and what next steps need to be taken. If you use an ASP version (application service providers) of such software, you, your local staff, and your telecommuting staff can use the same database. The call report can be invaluable in future years, especially if there is a change in personnel.

What are call reports and why are they used?

After a meeting with a major gift prospect, or after any cultivation step, it is important to document any important information you gathered during the visit. This helps maintain an ongoing record on each major gift prospect and gives valuable information for future visits. A useful way of recording this information is through the use of a *call report*—a simple form that can be filled out easily following the visit (see Exhibit 8.3). The upper part of the form is where you record specific prospect contact information, the name of the staff person making the contact, and the date of the visit.

EXHIBIT 8.3.   SAMPLE CALL REPORT FORM.

Name of Prospect _____   Volunteer or Staff Member _____
Address _____   Date of Contact _____
Telephone Number _____
Fax Number _____
E-Mail Address _____

Type of Contact: _____

Purpose:

Outcome and Results:

Pertinent Information Determined:

Next Step?   By When?

Signature _____   Date _____

Please complete and return to the director of development within three days of visit.

The lower part of the form is where you record the specific visit information (responses are in parentheses):

What type of contact was it? (By telephone, a personal visit, a chance encounter?)

What was the purpose of the visit? (To provide information the prospect requested, to find out more about the prospect's interests, to ask for a major gift of $50,000?)

What was the outcome? (Prospect asked for additional information about our organization, or the prospect said she needs to talk to her accountant before making a decision.)

Was there any pertinent information determined?

Next step? By when? (This is a very important part of the call report because it sets the time frame for the next contact with the prospect—it could be as simple as "call the prospect by [date] or "visit again in three months to keep her informed of our programs").

The reports are then filed in a prospect's individual file or recorded in your database tracking system. The important point is to keep these forms current. They are the historical record of a prospect's involvement with your organization, and they will provide useful information for staff members in the future. Some fundraising software programs now have call report features that make it much easier to record the information right in the prospect's electronic record.

I am trying to revamp our major gift clubs. Should I offer premiums?

Many organizations do not offer premiums for the major gift membership organizations. They might offer premiums for their direct mail donors, but at the higher levels of giving, they generally offer a premium listing in the annual donor honor roll and perhaps a donor recognition dinner the night before a big football game or concert. We do know of one institution that gives major gift donors commemorative pottery, but they do not market it during the solicitation. Therefore it does not become a required gesture.

Making a personal stewardship visit, in which you thank the donor for support and update him or her on the impact of the donation on your organization, is one of the most effective forms of recognition and stewardship for major donors.

How do I handle mailing deadlines that conflict with the holidays?

Let's say your annual Major Donor Weekend event is set for March 12 through 14. You typically send out formal invitations three months in advance, so people have time to make travel arrangements. This has you sending the invitations just before Christmas, and you are afraid they will get caught up in all the Christmas mail. How do you handle this?

Two approaches might work. One is to send the reminder in late November and include a special "we are thankful for you" message with a "save the date" message. The other is to wait to send out the save-the-date until the first week of the New Year. It will be in the post-Christmas rush but still a time when people are not as caught up in their usual schedules. Making personal telephone calls to your largest donors is a great way to personalize the invitations.

Is it a good idea to have group dinners, lunches, and other such events as a way to cultivate major donors?

One secret to cultivating major donors is creating an environment in which they feel comfortable learning more about your organization, want to ask questions, and, most importantly, can be made to feel as if they are insiders to your plans and vision. Make sure you are not creating an environment in which potential major donors feel as though they are being sold something.

To prevent this and do a better job of cultivations, set up a schedule of regular personal visits to keep potential major donors informed of special programs, upcoming projects, or news from your organization.

You might develop an "insiders' newsletter" for your top donors. This could be a special mailing of a letter from the CEO that outlines special news or developments before these go out to the public through the media.

Maintaining telephone contact is another easy method. Call people to thank them for their support and to let them know how their money has helped. Perhaps you'll have a special list of top donors who you will want to call on a special occasion, such as their birthday or their anniversary. And for those who are interested, be sure to include major donors and prospects on volunteer committees at your organization.

Volunteers can be involved in these types of cultivation activities, and each of these methods helps you to categorize your major gift donors into manageable groups and to become more effective in strengthening relationships between the donor and the organization.

How can I sell a major donor on the idea of giving enough to rename our facility in his honor?

How you make this approach will depend on how involved the donor is with your organization. If the donor is not very familiar with your organization, we suggest that you have two or more separate meetings with him. The first meeting should focus on learning more about the donor, and the donor learning more about your organization. If the donor has to learn about your organization's mission and strategic plan during the solicitation, it is not time to solicit.

Ideally, the donor is already involved with your organization, has been a long-time donor, and is serving on the board or a committee. In this case, the presentation should focus on the donor's vision for the organization's future and how that vision can become a reality with this gift. In other words, the presentation needs to be about the donor more than the organization. Sell the results of the gift and how it will positively affect other people's lives.

Before you determine the amount that would rename the facility, have your development committee make a recommendation to your board about what size gift would be appropriate. Once this recommendation is made, the board should discuss and approve it, and then there should be no negotiation with donors regarding the amount.

Before determining the amount, consider the following factors: the value of the naming opportunity should be high, because you can only do it once; it should be enough to meet some long-term need of the organization, not just fix an immediate budget problem; and it should be one of the largest gifts your organization has ever received.

Summary

Major gifts programs are the hallmark of successful fundraising at large organizations. You should have learned in this chapter techniques and strategies to position your institution to identify, engage, and solicit large gifts on an ongoing basis. Simply put, you want to engage those donors capable of making major gifts personally in the mission of what you are trying to accomplish.

CHAPTER NINE

CAPITAL CAMPAIGNS: BUILDING SUCCESS

Capital campaigns are important events in the lives of both the organizations and the fundraisers who work in them. A capital campaign occurs once every ten years or so for many organizations and once in a lifetime for some smaller organizations. Much like running for political office, once you have embarked on a campaign, your life and your organization's life will never be the same. That is why it is so important to have a clear understanding of how to conduct the campaign properly and to do everything in your power to make it a success.

The professional fundraiser's primary role in a capital campaign is to educate, motivate, organize, and most importantly, focus volunteer leadership. Successful capital campaigns require volunteer leaders to conduct face-to-face solicitations for major gifts. However, in our experience, many volunteers want to do everything but face-to-face solicitations. We have had volunteers take up entire meetings talking about golf tournaments, benefit concerts, government grants, and many other ideas to avoid having to make face-to-face solicitations. Whether you are working with a consultant or not, remember your most important job in a capital campaign is keeping volunteer leaders focused.

In this chapter you will learn about what a capital campaign is, how to get ready for the campaign, how best to use a consultant, what you should expect from a feasibility study, and what to do and watch out for when events do not go exactly according to plan. You will find answers to the following questions in this chapter:

- How do I prepare my organization for a successful capital campaign?
- How does a capital campaign differ from a comprehensive campaign?
- What are the reasons to hire a consultant to help with a capital campaign?
- What should be included in a capital campaign feasibility study?
- If a feasibility study reveals that a board's top priority is unpopular, should I still proceed with the project?
- What is the difference between a case summary, a case for support, and a case statement?
- What are some pointers for writing a case statement or case for support?
- What is the appropriate way to ask someone to chair a capital campaign and when should it be done?
- What do you do with a stalled capital campaign?
- Will a capital campaign negatively affect annual giving?
- What are the major pitfalls to avoid in a capital campaign?
- How can my organization's capital campaign help my career?
- How should planned gifts be counted in a capital or comprehensive campaign?
- What percentage of pledges can we expect to be paid?
- Do you have any hard and fast rules for when to break ground for a building? Can we still raise money after groundbreaking?

How do I prepare my organization for a successful capital campaign?

Proper preparation is a key to a successful campaign. By assisting your organization in putting the following items in place, you will ensure that your campaign will have a greater likelihood of success.

1. A shared vision of what the organization could be if all of its long-range plans were achieved
2. An organization financial plan that clearly shows the realistic role of philanthropy
3. A compelling, written case statement that articulates the rationale for private, philanthropic support
4. People willing and able to serve as volunteer campaign leaders who can recruit others to work on the campaign and ask for major gift support
5. An internal audit of the fundraising program to ensure that systems are in place to support the campaign effort
6. An external feasibility study that helps test the case for support and identifies potential leaders and gifts necessary to raise 40 to 60 percent of the total campaign goal
7. A Range of Gifts Chart that shows the size and number of gifts needed for a successful campaign

8. Commitment of 100 percent of the board to support the capital campaign financially
9. Realistic expectation that there is one gift available that could equal 20 percent of the total goal
10. Staff with the ability to provide adequate support to campaign volunteers
11. Written agreement on campaign accounting policies and named gift opportunities
12. An appropriate budget for campaign expenses
13. A written campaign plan
14. An agreement that the campaign will not be publicly announced until a large portion of the goal (over 80 percent) is achieved and all major prospects are personally solicited

How does a capital campaign differ from a comprehensive campaign?

A *capital campaign* is a volunteer-lead fundraising effort for a specific building or capital project that has a defined time period and secures cash pledges generally payable over three to five years. Capital campaigns are usually conducted in addition to an organization's annual fundraising efforts.

Comprehensive campaigns, on the other hand, typically include all giving to an organization over time. For example, if an institution is normally raising $5 million per year, and the campaign pledge period is five years, then an additional $25 million is added to the overall campaign goal. Some comprehensive campaigns go a next step and also include planned or deferred gifts in campaign goals. This practice has lead to even larger goals and, in some cases, campaign accounting abuses.

Generally, the comprehensive campaign is better suited for larger institutions that have mature annual giving programs and planned giving efforts that yield a steady flow of commitments. Smaller organizations are better served by focusing on their capital needs and not including all giving in a comprehensive campaign.

When smaller organizations approach their first capital campaign, they are often challenged by how to ask a donor to make a normal annual gift and a capital campaign pledge on top of it. There is no perfect way to accomplish this dual "ask," but one way is to solicit the capital pledge and make sure you tell the donor that they will be solicited for their annual fund gift in the same manner as in years past.

What are the reasons to hire a consultant to help with a capital campaign?

A capital campaign that begins poorly usually ends poorly. No matter what the size of your campaign goal, there are reasons to consider hiring an experienced consultant to help with a capital campaign.

For example, if your organization has never done a capital campaign, your staff and volunteers might need an outside, experienced voice to provide strategy and direction. Or if your development staff does not have experience running and developing strategy for capital campaigns, you might need access to someone who does. This is especially true if your development staff also needs to focus on annual giving.

You also might find that at times your volunteer leadership, and your board, will need an outside voice to get started or to stay focused. Sometimes a consultant can motivate and focus volunteers in ways that staff cannot.

We were reminded of this point at a capital campaign meeting for a new museum honoring an American pop music icon. Staff had organized this prospect assignment meeting with the hope that at the conclusion all of the major prospects would have been assigned to a volunteer team for face-to-face solicitation. Staff brought prospect lists for the volunteers to review and discuss. At the start of the meeting, the campaign chair explained the correct purpose of the meeting: to evaluate and select prospects for solicitation. Then, in no particular order, the volunteers brought up all sorts of ideas: Can we get a musical CD made and sell it to raise money? Can we get a number of celebrities to do a benefit concert? Maybe we should try to get more government funding. On and on they went.

Each time a different idea was presented, the campaign consultant had to remind the volunteers that face-to-face solicitation was the most effective and efficient form of fundraising and focus them back on the activities that would raise the needed major gifts for the campaign.

Other reasons you might need a consultant include the following:

- You are not sure who will provide the volunteer leadership to your campaign and will make key recruitments and solicitations.
- You need someone who has experience writing campaign case statements and campaign marketing materials.
- You need someone who has experience developing named gift opportunities and Range of Gift Tables.
- You need someone who can help keep an inexperienced organization from developing strategies that are ineffective and time consuming.

If your campaign goal is small (under $2 million) you will not need a full-time resident consultant, and you might only need to have a consultant help you with preparations for the campaign by conducting a feasibility study. This type of study identifies your top leadership and your top gifts, helps you articulate your case for support, and helps you develop your overall campaign strategy. Most importantly, this type of study helps to ensure that your campaign starts off in the proper direction.

We can tell too many tales of organizations that start their campaigns without the assistance of a study or sound strategy. (Remember, hope is not a strategy.) Often they raise 40 percent of their goal really quickly, and they are really excited about how it is going, and then slowly but surely the campaign stalls, and they cannot get it moving beyond that mark. As it drags on and on, the organization has an almost permanent sense of failure when it comes to the campaign. A failed campaign can haunt an organization for ten to fifteen years.

Whether you hire a consultant or not, be sure you must have a sound strategy from the beginning. Take as much time as needed to identify, cultivate, solicit, and secure your top gifts before announcing the campaign or soliciting too many people. Get gifts from 100 percent of your board members and look to get major gifts from at least one-third of your board. Have a prospect list that is 90 percent or more individuals, corporations, and foundations that are already involved and supporting your organization and 10 percent new ones.

What should be included in a capital campaign feasibility study?

While some might argue otherwise, in our experience, there is no standard outline for a feasibility study. Every consulting firm seems to have a somewhat different approach to them.

However, there are some things that you should expect from a study. First, the study should involve interviews with your top campaign prospects and potential leadership. Staff and volunteers should be involved in the process of identifying people to be interviewed. A case statement should be written for use in the interviews, and an initial Range of Gifts Chart should be developed as well.

You should expect to receive a written report that includes a section of findings that reports to you what interviewees said and any trends that developed during the course of the study. These should be broken down into subcategories that include reactions to your case for support, suggestions for campaign leadership, and potential lead gifts identified during the study. Be suspicious of findings that rely heavily on percentages, such as "80 percent of those surveyed said they would consider a gift to the campaign."

This type of finding can be misleading because a large percentage of capital campaign contributions will come from a small number of the donors. If the few who said they would not consider giving are also the ones who have all the money, this statistic could mislead you into a campaign doomed to failure.

You should also expect to find a section of recommendations. The recommendations section should be the bulk of the report and should provide you with specific campaign strategies in all of the areas in which findings were reported, based on an analysis of those findings.

You should also expect to find appendixes that include such things as an organization chart for the campaign, Range of Gifts Table for the recommended goal, volunteer job descriptions, and a preliminary budget.

Most importantly, the study should provide you with specific next steps to initiate a campaign and outline the strategy to secure the top gifts that will be needed for success.

If a feasibility study reveals that a board's top priority is unpopular, should I still proceed with the project?

It depends on how you define *constituents*. If constituents are your potential lead donors who can make a difference in the campaign's success, then you should rethink your next steps in the campaign. Find out (from the person who did the study) who was the most opposed to the project. Then arrange for board members to make personal visits with each of the people opposed to the project (who are potential large donors) to explain to them why the project is important.

Often people (especially major donors) will be negative about projects that they have not had an opportunity to influence or discuss. In our experience, money follows involvement. Given time to learn more about the project and discuss their thoughts personally with board members, their opposition might fade (or the board members might rethink the priority). After this process, your board can then decide if the campaign should go forward and where these prospects stand as far as their support.

If it turns out, however, that the potential lead donors were positive about the project, but many others were not, you might want to proceed with the early phases of your campaign while seeking to involve more constituents in discussions about the importance of this new building project.

What is the difference between a case summary, a case for support, and a case statement?

The campaign *case summary* is a preliminary three- to five-page document that is sent to those potential campaign leaders and donor prospects that agreed to be interviewed in the feasibility study. Its purpose is to acquaint them with your organization and the details of your proposed campaign.

The campaign case summary precedes the visit of the fundraising consultant. This allows the prospect time to process the campaign information prior to the consultant's visit, be more prepared to offer advice on the proposed campaign, and answer the consultant's questions.

The case summary can be viewed as a miniversion of the case statement that will be used during the campaign. The case summary needs to be brief, to ensure the interviewees actually take the time to read it; yet it must contain all the details of the campaign: background about your organization, reasons for the campaign, the proposed campaign budget, and descriptions of how the money will be used.

The case summary should be visionary and action-oriented. It justifies the campaign to the reader and inspires thought about how the campaign can be successful and what role the reader should play.

The campaign *case statement* (or *case for support*) helps volunteers represent an organization to its donor base. It is the essential document of the campaign: not only is it a tool volunteers can refer to as they make their calls, but it will be left behind with major donors for subsequent reference and review before they make their final decision.

The case statement should contain all the facts and figures relevant to the campaign, since it will also serve the staff or campaign manager as a graphic and textual reference point for subsequent marketing materials (the major gift brochure, gift opportunities brochure, proposals, and even annual fund appeals).

It too needs to be visionary and action-oriented. It justifies the campaign to readers and inspires them not only to support the organization with a major gift but also to act as an advocate with others.

What are some pointers for writing a case statement or case for support?

A proven format, developed by the national consulting firm of Alexander Haas Martin & Partners, shows us that the first page of the case statement is read most carefully, like the lead paragraphs of a newspaper article. Pack information into the first few paragraphs and get the "ask" right up front, preferably on what will become the first or second page of the case when produced, before you risk losing your reader. The first few paragraphs of the case should establish the organization's mission and credentials and briefly state the crisis that has necessitated the campaign.

Remember that a sense of urgency is important; incorporate it early in the case. Sell opportunity, not need. Donors want to make a difference. Your case should tell them how they can influence the world by making an investment in your organization, not how to help you build more office space.

Once you have passionately explained the importance and urgency of the opportunity, then make the "ask." Use boldface type. When the case is formatted and produced, these key lead paragraphs should appear on the first or second page.

If possible, lead into the case text with a profile of an individual that your organization serves, statistics that dramatize the immensity of the problem your organization is trying to help solve, or another dramatic device that will ensure the reader's undivided attention.

The next section is informal: it should set forth the history and distinctive competency of the organization: its mission, programs, and community support.

Next, provide details of the campaign. State the organization's plans for change through campaign funding:

- State the needs the campaign will address.
- Outline the careful and responsible planning process used to determine the projects.
- Tell your audience how their money will be spent (programs, capital expenditures, endowment for support, and so on).
- Document costs for capital projects. Describe each and how it will deliver services or solve a problem.
- Get the prospective donor involved by showing how a gift can effect organizational change and benefit people. (How many more will be served if a new building is built? Can the program be replicated so that it will serve children throughout the state?)
- Emphasize the organization's vision for the future and how the campaign can secure it.
- Last, briefly restate your organization's mission and how the campaign will enhance it. Pitch a final, urgent "ask." Make the voice of the last section a more intimate, emotional *I* or *you* (or, even better, *"together, we can make this happen"*).

End with a dollar summary of the campaign goals, information about the length of the campaign, and vehicles for gift giving. Include the names and phone numbers of the volunteer leadership and the executive director.

What is the appropriate way to ask someone to chair a capital campaign and when should it be done?

Recruiting a capital campaign chair needs to be done face-to-face or not at all. As the following example from Kristina's experience shows, recruiting the right person to lead your capital campaign needs to be done personally.

After some preliminary interviews with various candidates, we were convinced we had the right chair. He could give a lead gift both personally and corporately; he was personally involved with the organization; and, as CEO of a Fortune 500 company, he had access to many potential major donors.

We presented our findings to the executive director. He reviewed the candidate's list and our recommendations. He was pleased with our selection because he personally knew this individual. In the midst of the meeting, he immediately started to draft a letter to the candidate. We all assumed it was to request a meeting. He finished the draft, had his secretary type it, and sent it around for our review. We were shocked. The letter did not request a meeting. It was the request to the candidate to chair the campaign.

We immediately set up another meeting with the executive director to explain that he would have to meet the candidate in person. We tried every argument possible, but the executive director insisted that he was too busy to meet the candidate in person. (Maybe that should have been our first warning.) Besides, the executive director argued, it was a poor use of resources to travel all that way for one meeting. In spite of all our arguments to the contrary, the executive director mailed his letter.

Should anyone be surprised that a letter came back, within a few days, respectfully declining the invitation to serve as campaign chair? Of course, we did not get a lead gift from that individual either. Fortunately for the campaign, the executive director decided that he would start going to see people in person when he had something important to ask.

Generally, you should recruit the chair as early in the campaign planning process as possible. Once you have established your projects and goals and have conducted a feasibility study, you should be in a position to recruit the campaign chair. However, if the potential chair has had limited involvement with your organization, you might need to take additional steps before conducting the recruitment. These steps might include completing your board campaign and getting a flooring gift or two.

When actually making the recruitment, have a summary of the campaign objectives and a job description (such as in Exhibit 9.1) that show what you want the chair to do. Be aware that most potential leaders might say that they are too busy when their real question is, "Will this campaign be successful?" Be prepared to answer this question by sharing the results of your feasibility study or by securing one or two large gifts before recruiting the campaign chair.

What do you do with a stalled capital campaign?

One of our members wrote to tell us that she had been attempting to wrap up the final portion of a $1.2 million dollar capital campaign that started five years ago. She had been unable to raise the final $250,000 after two years of effort, and she was looking for ideas on how to find new prospects.

To make matters worse, she ended up taking out a short-term loan that the organization had to renew every six months. Their total operating budget was just over $400,000, with approximately 85 percent coming from private contributions. The campaign was almost entirely carried out by volunteers and staff. They did not hire a campaign consultant, nor did they have a development director.

EXHIBIT 9.1. CAPITAL CAMPAIGN CHAIR
JOB DESCRIPTION.

Campaign Chair

The campaign chair is critical to the success of the campaign. The chair provides over-all volunteer leadership, recruits committee leadership, participates in general cam-paign planning and specific solicitation strategies, and motivates volunteers.

Specifically, the chair will perform the following duties:

- Assist in identifying and recruiting ten to fifteen volunteers to serve on the cam-paign steering committee. These individuals must be willing to solicit three to five campaign prospects.
- Approve the campaign plan (strategy) and case statement.
- Attend and conduct campaign steering committee meetings.
- Meet with support staff and campaign counsel for an update on campaign activ-ities and strategic decisions on next steps.
- Solicit four to five prospects in the $50,000 to $300,000 range for flooring phase of the campaign.
- Acknowledge gifts and pledges as they are received (letters prepared by support staff) and sign other appropriate campaign correspondence.
- Perform other duties to help ensure campaign success.
- Make a leadership gift to the campaign.

This is a good example of a stalled campaign. Like many people stuck in stalled campaigns, this person was looking for new donors to help. Imagine that, as a prospective donor, you have never given to an organization, and now you are asked to help finish off a struggling, unsuccessful project that has debt attached to it. Are you eager to write a check?

When faced with a stalled campaign, the ideal thing to do is to find a chal-lenge grant. Review the list of donors and look for a person (or persons) who could offer a challenge grant to complete the campaign. For example, could someone pledge $50,000 dollars as a challenge to all donors to raise an additional $200,000? Alternatively, could three or four donors pledge $125,000 to be matched on a one-to-one basis, for a total of $250,000?

With a challenge gift in hand, it is a lot easier to ask donors to help meet a challenge than to ask them to help finish a struggling, unsuccessful, debt-ridden campaign. In other words, you can stop referring to it as a stalled campaign and start talking about meeting the challenge.

With a challenge you could ask donors to give again: one relatively easy way to accomplish this would be to ask the donors to simply extend their pledges one more year. This is a somewhat painless way for a donor to increase a pledge.

The challenge would also give you a stronger opportunity to go back to donors who underdonated or refused the first campaign request.

Will a capital campaign negatively affect annual giving?

A well-run campaign should not adversely affect your annual fundraising efforts, but without the right strategy, it can. We once had a potential client tell us that they were going to postpone their annual campaign while they did their capital campaign. Their logic was that they had a small board and a small pool of potential volunteers who could make face-to-face solicitations. Plus they thought their donors would rather give to a building project instead of operations. (So would we—which is why we recommend talking about funding your mission instead of funding operations when doing annual fund campaigns.)

This type of thinking is driven by the belief that people will only give once a year to an organization, that donors do not understand the need for both capital and annual investments, and that donors' first gifts will be their biggest. All of these are incorrect assumptions that carry with them the danger that you will send the message to your donors that you only need their support for capital projects, not day-to-day operations.

To avoid this thinking, the capital campaign strategy needs to include the philosophy that annual fund gifts will be protected as part of the capital campaign and that a capital gift is a pledge that is over and above the donors' normal giving. (The next time you are sitting in a church that asks for an offering, think about how many times a year people give in response to an "ask.") Volunteers need to be trained to communicate this to donors, and in the case of your larger annual donors you might want to solicit their capital campaign pledge and their current-year annual pledge at the same time with the understanding that you will also be asking for their annual support in future years.

What are the major pitfalls to avoid in a capital campaign?

There are several things that can go wrong in a campaign, and once they happen they are difficult to correct. The first mistake that many (perhaps most) campaigns make is to announce their campaigns too early. There is generally a sense of urgency among leaders to get the word out about the campaign. However, this is totally contradictory to sound capital campaign strategy.

Capital campaigns should focus on one-on-one communication with top donors and treat them as insiders to the campaign process. Your major prospective donors should not be reading about your campaign in the local paper before they are asked to contribute to its success.

The second biggest mistake made in capital campaigns is the failure to get accurate construction costs for the capital projects. Many times the cost-estimating process is done superficially.

Make sure that significant effort is put into conceptualizing the design of the project before the campaign begins and that accurate cost estimates are secured. The last thing you want is to exceed your campaign goal and then not be able to deliver what has been promoted in the campaign case statement.

The third mistake that can be disastrous for a capital campaign is to develop a strategy that is going to rely on broad-based participation for its success. The "if we could get a thousand people to give us $1,000 each" philosophy is a guaranteed prescription for failure. You must rely on large gifts for your success and try to get at least one gift to equal 20 percent of your goal and the top ten gifts to equal 40 to 60 percent of the total goal.

There are other things to watch out for, including lack of CEO involvement in the campaign, beginning construction before the campaign is completed, lack of board support early in the effort, not asking for specific amounts in the solicitations, and not having an adequate campaign budget.

How can my organization's capital campaign help my career?

A successful campaign can be the watermark of your career. As you consider other positions, one of the things that will be the focal point for evaluating your strengths as a candidate will be your experience in successful capital campaigns. In fact, many times a search for a new chief development officer is done in anticipation of a capital campaign, and your successful experience in a prior campaign could be pivotal to enhancing your fundraising career.

Search firms seeking top-level candidates for positions will often look to institutions and organizations that have had successful capital campaigns for their job candidate pool. In addition, more and more job qualifications include capital campaign experience as one of the criteria for hiring. Therefore being an integral part of or leading a successful capital campaign is one of the best things for anyone's career in fundraising.

How should planned gifts be counted in a capital or comprehensive campaign?

First, one of the issues that fundraising professionals will face in working on large capital campaigns is the issue of campaign accounting. A thorough understanding of campaign accounting issues is very important to your career. The short answer to the question is that planned gifts should be counted at their present value. The Council for Advancement and Support of Education (CASE) and the Association of Fundraising Professionals (AFP) have adopted policies that suggest that campaigns should report both current value and face value of planned gifts. Our advice is to report only present value and not face value of planned gifts. Using face value numbers can work to inflate campaign goals falsely. Whatever you decide, it is best to establish reporting guidelines (such as those presented in Exhibit 9.2) at the beginning of your campaign and to ask the campaign leadership to approve these guidelines.

EXHIBIT 9.2.   CAPITAL CAMPAIGN MODEL REPORTING GUIDELINES.

I.   Purpose and Scope

The purpose of these guidelines is to establish a common understanding among donors, volunteers, and staff as to how gifts should be valued and reported for campaign purposes. The guidelines cover situations commonly encountered in a capital campaign. Unusual circumstances should be referred to the campaign steering committee serving as the gift acceptance committee for the campaign. The committee should develop responses based on these guidelines, industry practices, and, if appropriate, tax laws and regulations.

II.   Principles and Definitions

A.   Gifts and pledges may be counted in only one campaign.

B.   The value of any cancelled or unfulfilled pledges should be subtracted from campaign totals when it is determined they will not be realized.

C.   If a planned gift previously reported in the campaign matures during the campaign period, the amount reported as a planned gift is cancelled, and the matured gift is reported as an outright gift.

D.   The value of a gift for campaign purposes may vary from the tax deduction value (if any) or the value used in recording the gift on financial statements.

E.   Fair Market Value: "The price at which the property would change hands between a willing buyer and a willing seller, neither being under any compulsion to buy or sell and both having a reasonable knowledge of relevant facts." (IRS regulations.)

F.   Government Funding: Government grants and allocations should be considered on a case-by-case basis for reporting in campaign totals. It is the philosophy of the campaign that government funding, whether from a local, state, or federal entity, should only be included in the campaign if the funds are triggered by a philanthropic event. Under this principle, grants or appropriations from governmental bodies to the campaign's featured objectives are eligible for campaign credit. State or federal matching grants earned on the basis of raising funds from private gifts and grants are also eligible for campaign credit.

III. Time Periods

A. Campaign Period: [MM/DD/YY] through [MM/DD/YY] is the period during which pledges and gifts will be accepted and reported in campaign totals. At the conclusion of the board, flooring, and lead gift phases of the campaign, the definition of the campaign period may be reconsidered.

B. Pledge Period: The length of the payment period for pledges is [x] years (or [x] tax years or [x] months, normally not exceeding five years). The pledge period should be reconsidered at the major and final phases of the campaign and may be shortened to [Y] years (usually three years).

IV. Pledges

A. Accepting and Recording Pledges: To be included in campaign totals, a commitment must be written, signed by the donor, and received by the campaign office. This is usually accomplished by completing a campaign letter of intent, pledge card, or equivalent. Documentation must commit the donor to a specific dollar amount that should be paid according to a fixed time schedule, usually the pledge period.

B. "Reported Not Confirmed" (RNC): Not a pledge, "reported not confirmed" is a notation used to track prospects who have made a verbal commitment to the campaign but have not yet provided written documentation. Usually, an RNC is followed by a written pledge, which is signed by the donor and contains all necessary details. The pledge can then be included in campaign totals. In rare cases, an official of the campaign must facilitate the conversion of an RNC into an acceptable pledge by sending a confirmation letter to the donor. The confirmation letter details the terms of the pledge and asks the donor to return the letter with his or her signature to confirm the pledge. When the campaign office receives the donor-signed confirmation letter, the pledge should be included in campaign totals.

C. FASB Statement No. 116: Statement No. 116, issued by the Financial Accounting Standards Board, prescribes rules for recognizing and reporting contributions on audited financial statements. FASB 116 is built on the concept that a gift is an unconditional, voluntary, nonreciprocal transfer of assets (including unconditional promises) to a not-for-profit organization. A promise, according to FASB, is an irrevocable commitment by the donor to the institution. This notion of a promise differs from a statement of intent, which is retractable. It is the position of [name of organization] that campaign letters of intent are statements of intent and are therefore not subject to the requirements of FASB 116.

D. Extended Pledges: An extended pledge has a payment schedule that exceeds the pledge period. The payments received during the pledge period will be reported as a normal gift. The payments in the "extra" years should be reported and discounted at net present value using a 4 percent discount rate from the first year of the pledge. The calculations can be made using a financial calculator or a computer spreadsheet.

(Continued)

EXHIBIT 9.2. Continued.

To give an example, a donor makes a ten-year pledge of $10,000 per year. The campaign has a five-year pledge period and uses a 4 percent discount rate for extended pledges. The first five years are reported at face value ($50,000). The second five years are reported at $36,591 in the campaign total. This amount is the net present value at year one of the pledge or the payments made in years six through ten of the pledge. The total value reported for the pledge is $86,591 (the sum of $50,000 and $36,591).

V. *Fulfilling Pledges*

A. Basic Concepts
   1. If planned gifts are included in the campaign, the campaign should report separate totals for outright gifts, planned gifts, and the total campaign.
   2. Gifts that will be completed during the pledge period are considered outright gifts. Outright gifts should be accepted for the fulfillment of pledges for any featured objective of the campaign.
   3. Planned gifts are those expected to be completed after the conclusion of the pledge period. Planned gifts may be accepted for the fulfillment of pledges for endowment purposes.

B. Outright Gifts
   1. Cash: Checks must be made out to [organization's official name used on checks] and not to an individual representing the campaign.
   2. Marketable Securities: Gifts of marketable securities—on a stock exchange or in the over-the-counter market—will be valued at the mean of the high and low quoted selling prices on the date the donor relinquished control of the assets in favor of [short form name] or trust. For some bonds and certain securities traded in the over-the-counter market, the mean of the bid and the "ask" is used to value the gift. In accordance with standard gift reporting guidelines, neither losses nor gains realized on the sale of the stock by [short form name], nor brokerage fees or other expenses associated with the transaction, should affect the reported gift value.
   3. Mutual Fund Shares: Mutual fund shares will be valued at their public redemption price on the date of the gift. If there is no such quotation for the fund on the date of the gift (for example, because the gift is made on a Saturday, Sunday, or holiday), the campaign should report the shares at the previous public redemption price quoted by the fund.
   4. Interest in a Closely Held Business: The gift acceptance committee will consider gifts of interests in closely held businesses (corporation, partnership, limited liability company) on a case-by-case basis. Because the income they generate might subject [name of organization] to Unrelated Business Income Tax (UBIT), gifts of S Corporations will be subject to additional

scrutiny. Gifts of closely held business interest exceeding $10,000 will be reported at the fair market value placed on them by a qualified independent appraiser as required by the IRS for valuing gifts of stocks that are not publicly traded. Typically, this value can be obtained from IRS Form 8283, on which the donor must obtain the donee's signature for such gifts.

Gifts of closely held business interest valued at $10,000 or less may be valued at the per-share cash purchase price of the most recent transaction. If no redemption is made during the campaign period, such a gift may be reported at the value placed on the shares by an independent certified public account that audits the books for business.

5. Real and Personal Property: The gift acceptance committee will consider gifts of real and personal property on a case-by-case basis. Gifts of real and personal property that qualify as a charitable deduction for a donor should be valued at the fair market value. Gifts of real estate are also subject to the [short form name's] real estate gift acceptance policy.

Gifts with fair market values exceeding $5,000 will be counted at the values placed on them by qualified independent appraisers, as required by the IRS for valuing noncash charitable contributions. Typically, this value can be obtained from IRS Form 8283, on which the donor must obtain the donee's signature for such gifts. Gifts of $5,000 and under may be reported at the value declared by the donor. IRS requirements for gift substantiation place the responsibility for valuing property gifts on the donor for tax deduction purposes.

6. Life Insurance: For insurance policies to be reported in the campaign, the donor must make [short form name] the owner and sole irrevocable beneficiary of the policy. For campaign reporting purposes, the value of the gift is the lesser of (1) the fair market value of the policy or (2) the donor's cost basis. The definition of cost basis is the cumulative net premiums paid by the policy owner as of the date of the gift. The donor should obtain this information from the insurance company. The definition of fair market value—which the donor can obtain from the insurance company on IRS Form 712—depends on the age and type of contract (see following).

   a) Paid Up Insurance Policies: Fair market value is the replacement cost of the policy—the amount that the insurer would charge for a single-premium contract of the same face amount on the life of a person of the same age as the insured.

   b) Existing Policies Not Fully Paid Up: Fair market value is "the interpolated terminal reserve" value of the policy on the date of the gift. This value is usually slightly more than the cash value of the policy. Unrestricted gifts made by the donor to [short form name] to cover future premiums will be reported at face value.

(Continued)

EXHIBIT 9.2.   Continued.

   c) New Policies: For policies issued within one year of the gift, the fair mar-
      ket value is the net premium paid (the gross premium reduced by any
      dividend received by the policy owner). Unrestricted gifts made by
      the donor to [short form name] to cover future premiums should be
      reported at face value.
   d) Realized Death Benefits: The insurance company's settlement amount
      for an insurance policy whose death benefits are realized during the
      campaign period, whether the policy is owned by [short form name]
      or not, should be counted in campaign totals. An adjustment to cam-
      paign reports might be necessary if the policy had previously been
      given and recorded in campaign totals.
 C. Planned Gifts
   1. Split Interest Gifts
      a) Charitable Remainder Unitrusts
      b) Charitable Remainder Annuity Trusts
      c) Pooled Income Funds (Delete this item if organization, either by itself or
         through a related organization, does not offer.)
      d) Charitable Gift Annuities

What percentage of pledges can we expect to be paid?

It is hard to have one rule to apply to cash flow for all campaigns. Some issues to
consider include the following:

- Are you approaching foundations or major donors who would be inclined to
  give all in one year and not over time?
- Will the active soliciting time of the campaign last more than one year? If so,
  it might actually take four years for pledges to be paid in full. For example, if you
  started the campaign in September 2000, but I am not solicited until July 2001,
  I will be paying until July 2004, but your donors solicited in 2000 will be paying through 2003. Some campaigns avoid this issue by saying that all pledge
  payments should be completed by a certain date.
- Most campaigns see the bulk of the dollars in the second year because the active
  soliciting time in the campaign usually takes a while to generate results.

   If we have to give percentages, we say it is close to 30 percent in the first year,
25 percent in the second year, 20 percent in the third year, 15 percent in the fourth
year, and 10 percent in the fifth year.
   One last thing to consider: it is good for staff to be concerned about cash flow
during a campaign, but campaign volunteers and leadership need to be focused

on the fundraising goal. Get the pledges, and the cash will come. If volunteers are to be involved in the financing of the project and cash flow issues, it is best to have separate groups of volunteers focused on financing.

Do you have any hard and fast rules for when to break ground for a building? Can we still raise money after groundbreaking?

We heard from an organization whose board maintained all along that they could break ground when they raised enough gifts and pledges for all the construction costs, even though endowment is a part of the campaign goal. There are others who think they should wait until they have the endowment piece too. We say: they have not technically raised all the money for the building project because they have not raised the endowment piece yet.

Our rule regarding how much to raise before groundbreaking is related as much to how many major gift prospects you still have outstanding as it is to what percentage of the dollars have been raised. We recommend, for example, that you not break ground until all of the prospects you think have the capacity to give $50,000 (or some amount relative to the size of your project) have been personally solicited.

Gifts of this size and larger will be more difficult without personal solicitation, and if you solicit gifts after the groundbreaking your likelihood of success will be diminished significantly. We cannot explain totally the phenomena that happen, but our experience is that once you break ground and celebrate your success very little serious fundraising takes place. So treat your outstanding prospects as insiders to the process and raise as much of the endowment as possible before breaking ground. Make sure your campaign plan emphasizes the need for this (see Exhibit 9.3).

EXHIBIT 9.3.   SAMPLE TABLE OF CONTENTS FOR A CAPITAL CAMPAIGN PLAN AND BUDGET.

The following is a table of contents for a capital campaign plan. Use these following points to create a plan illustrating campaign readiness, previous campaign experience, and overall strength when appropriate. In addition to a comprehensive plan, it is helpful to have a one- to two-page executive summary that can be shared on a regular basis with volunteer leadership.

I.   Background to Campaign
A.   Proposed role of staff and volunteers (board members and major donors in active membership) in campaign leadership, including steering committee

(Continued)

EXHIBIT 9.3.   Continued.

B.   Method whereby longtime donors will help achieve goal
C.   Past campaign experience of organization
D.   Suggestions from campaign feasibility study
E.   Accuracy of campaign timing to gather broad-based support from prospective donors in the community

II. Campaign Strategy
A.   Underlying philosophy of campaign
B.   Illustration of sequential fundraising
C.   Necessity for a proper floor
D.   Plan for personal solicitations
E.   Plan for solicitation of board of trustees
F.   Range of Gifts Table

III. Campaign Organization, Implementation of Solicitation Strategies, and Schedule
A.   Plan for board solicitation
B.   Flooring phase
C.   Lead gifts phase
D.   Major gifts phase
E.   Final phase (membership solicitation)
F.   Staff campaign
G.   Campaign organization chart

IV. Campaign Budget
(Appendixes)
A.   Campaign chair job description
B.   Campaign steering committee job description
C.   Campaign vice chair job description
D.   Lead gifts committee
E.   Expense categories
Personnel
    Campaign:
        Campaign manager
        Administrative assistant
    Creative services:
        Research, writing, and editing
        Design and production
    Production and printing:
        Case statement
        Board case

Personalized proposals
Stationary, envelopes, and labels
Miscellaneous (other printing)
Operations
Photocopies
Postage and courier
Supplies
Travel
Telephone
Meetings and luncheons
Miscellaneous (contingency)
Total fees and expenses:

Summary

In this chapter we have defined capital campaigns and suggested approaches for planning successful campaigns. We have been a part of hundreds of capital campaigns and find that the success of most hinges on three key factors:

1. Are there enough large gifts to create early campaign momentum and ensure success? In our experience, campaigns with a lead gift of a minimum of 20 percent of the goal are successful.
2. Is the board prepared to lead by example in their giving and soliciting?
3. Is there a campaign leader who will make a significant personal financial investment in the campaign and who can access others who are capable of doing the same?

One last thought: challenge grants are always a good strategy to bring momentum and enthusiasm to a capital campaign.

CHAPTER TEN

PLANNED GIVING: YOU CAN DO IT

In 1999, John Havens and Paul Schervish of Boston College's Social Welfare Research Institute released their projections that $41 trillion would be transferred via estates over the next fifty years and that $6 trillion of it would go to charity (Havens and Schervish, 1999). Since then, nonprofits throughout the United States have felt compelled to start endowments or planned giving programs in order to get their piece of this $6 trillion. For most, however, planned giving has remained a mystery or a series of failed attempts. This chapter seeks to solve the mystery and outline key techniques for securing planned gifts.

The first step toward solving the mystery is defining the term: *planning giving* comprises various types of bequests, trusts, annuities, and other charitable commitments requiring some type of legal document. Planned giving is also referred to as *gift planning, deferred giving,* and *estate planning.* Planned giving programs have similarities to other fundraising programs. Planned giving, for example, requires a relationship between the donor and the institution and a case for support that clearly shows the impact of a gift.

There are significant differences too. Planned gifts generally take much longer to secure than a capital campaign pledge, an annual fund check, or a special event ticket purchase. A planned gift almost always involves third parties: attorneys, trust officers, accountants, family advisors, and so on. Planned gifts are usually family decisions involving not only spouses but also children and other relatives and possibly business partners. Planned gifts generally are made from donors' assets rather than their income. It is for these reasons that a planned giving program must be crafted to fit the style and demographics of your constituency.

We are often asked for help in starting or bringing focus to a planned giving program. Our experience has been that young organizations should not start an aggressive planned giving program until they have a mature annual giving program and have over a number of years received major cash gifts from individual donors.

One young nonprofit we know tried to start a planned giving program without building a base of annual giving. In fact, their strategy was to build an endowment so that they could stop doing annual fundraising. However, it is an idealistic thought that is usually not supported by donors. It raises many questions about the future of the organization. Were the leaders "too lazy" to continue their annual fund? Did the organization only have a mission to survive at its current level? Were current donors uninterested in continuing to provide support to the organization? If private support was not needed each year, would the organization be as responsive to changes in the community and its constituents? Would the funds raised simply ensure that certain staff members would be employed forever?

There is an approach that can work for virtually every nonprofit that has been operating for ten years or longer. Assuming that you have a fundraising track record of solid annual gifts and some major gifts, the best way to begin a planned giving program is simply to ask supporters to include your organization in their estate plans through a charitable bequest. Donors easily understand that you are asking them to have a significant impact on your organization. Based on our research—and on reality—all of your donors will eventually die, and a bequest is a proven and relatively painless way for a donor to make a significant gift.

In addition to these ideas, this chapter will answer the following questions:

- We are a young charitable nonprofit. How do we begin a planned giving program?
- What are the key instruments in planned giving and how are they defined?
- What should our organization do with an unexpected gift from someone's estate?
- What is an endowment? How do we start an endowment campaign?
- What is the best way to set a goal for endowment?
- What is the recommended amount of endowment for a nonprofit? How do you articulate the need for endowment to a donor?
- Do you have a list of possible objections people might have to making an endowment gift, and appropriate responses?
- What standard wording is used to assure donors that their endowment gifts will be used for the purposes they were intended? Is there any from of contract?

- Where would I find guidelines for developing endowment spending policies?
- How do we get documentation from donors that we are included in their will?
- How do I justify the need for a planned giving staff member to my board?
- What is your opinion on asking college students to purchase life insurance policies leaving the college as the beneficiary?
- These days should an organization new to planned giving accept a $25,000 gift annuity?
- How should gifts of stock be handled?

We are a young charitable nonprofit. How do we begin a planned giving program?

The simplest way to start a planned giving program is to talk with your best prospects (such as board members and regular donors) about including your organization in their estate plans. This is a simple and straightforward strategy and gives you a base of people who are committed to your organization and have philanthropic intent as far as their estate is concerned. Once you have built up a base of bequest expectancies you can then begin a more in-depth program that would include marketing trusts and other planned giving vehicles to those donors who have already indicated support of your mission. Many organizations spend a lot of time and money creating fancy planned giving programs before they even know if they really have prospects for such. A simple way to get started is to include a response line on every gift response vehicle that says, "Please send me more information about including [name of organization] in my estate plan."

What are the key instruments in planned giving and how are they defined?

A *charitable gift annuity* is a simple contract between your organization and the donor in which, in exchange for cash or securities, the organization agrees to pay the donor a certain sum for the rest of the donor's life guaranteed by the full faith and credit of the organization. Gift annuities are often set up for as little as $10,000. The donor receives a current income tax deduction (not the entire amount, since the donor is getting payments back), and a portion of the income is tax free.

The *charitable remainder unitrust* (CRUT) is a legal instrument by which the donor puts cash, securities, or real estate in trust, which is then invested by the trustee (such as a bank or the foundation itself) with payments (calculated annually as a percentage of the value of the trust) for life or a certain number of years to the donor or the donor and another beneficiary. The donor receives a current income tax deduction, can avoid capital gains tax, and removes the asset from his or her estate.

For example, a donor might set up a charitable remainder unitrust with $100,000 of appreciated securities, with a 5 percent payout. Thus, the first year the donor would receive $5,000 in payments. If the trust earned 10 percent during the year ($10,000), it would then be worth $105,000 at the end of the first year after the $5,000 payout, and the next year's payout would be 5 percent of $105,000 or $5,250. Of course, the risk is that the investments could go the other way as well.

The *flip CRUT* is a way of converting a low-income, hard-to-market asset to a higher payout rate, which is steadier. Usually the flip CRUT is funded with real estate. At the beginning the CRUT only pays whatever income the asset earns. If it is raw land, this could be zero. When the real estate is sold, this triggers a change to a standard CRUT, with a fixed payout percentage. At this point, the trust assets are invested in stocks and bonds. The flip is from an income-only CRUT to a standard CRUT. You could say it's a way of providing someone who is "land poor" with a better stream of income. The capital gains on the sale of the land are deferred. Charities are the beneficiaries of the CRUT and get the remainder when the trust matures, usually at the death of the beneficiary (or beneficiaries). So this is a pretty good deal for the charities, too. They usually get stocks and bonds and not the real estate, which is messy to deal with.

A *pooled income fund* is a trust designed to provide variable yet reliable income. Like a commercial mutual fund, it combines a donor's gift with the contributions of other fund participants, wisely investing the sum for a balance of income and growth. Dividends are paid to the shareholders in proportion to each person's contribution. Each donor's donation results in a tax deduction for the year the gift was made, an elimination of capital gains tax if they invest appreciated securities, and a reduction of estate taxes for their heirs.

What should our organization do with an unexpected gift from someone's estate?

Even if your organization has never received a substantial, unexpected gift as the result of someone leaving your organization in his or her will, it is wise to put in place a policy about the use of surprise gifts. We worked with an organization a few years ago that kept spending surprise gifts and kept adding to its operating budget as a result. One year they did not receive any surprise gifts, and all of the sudden they had a budget deficit of $500,000. Involve your development committee in discussions about such a policy and have them recommend to your board that any unrestricted bequest received will be placed as part of the permanent endowment of your organization. Many donors will designate the use of their funds, but your policy should strictly address unrestricted money.

What is an endowment? How do we start an endowment campaign?

An *endowment* is a permanent fund that is invested such that a portion of the annual income produced is used for operations or other specified purposes. It is created for the permanent upkeep and benefit of an institution or organization.

The formation of a sustainable nonprofit organization can be a long and complex process. Grass-roots community groups evolve into formal, staffed organizations, which can become established and evolve into institutions. During this transition, the focus evolves from satisfying fundamental needs (keeping the bills paid) to securing the long-term operation and stability of the organization (creating an endowment). Concerning the latter, governing boards might create an endowment or conduct special endowment campaigns.

To succeed in an endowment campaign, organizations must have first passed through a number of growth phases and have developed the characteristics of a mature organization. Does your organization meet the criteria? Here are nine simple questions to help you determine if your organization is positioned for endowment campaign success (provided to us by Alexander Haas Martin & Partners, www.ahmp.com).

1. Do you have a committed board that readily gives and solicits funds for your organization on a regular basis and is prepared to give significant and sacrificial gifts to an endowment campaign?
2. Do you have a track record of success in major fundraising campaigns, and have you demonstrated proper stewardship through the completion of the projects proposed during those campaigns?
3. Do you have eight to ten current donors who are capable and prepared to give between 80 and 90 percent of the endowment campaign goal?
4. Do you have a long history of financial stability and conservative fiscal management?
5. Can you justify the need for an endowment and show how endowment-generated income will enable you to better serve your constituents? (Remember, for every $1 million in your endowment, you will typically only receive $50,000 in annual income.)
6. Have you developed a detailed long-range plan and satisfied all other pressing and foreseeable capital and programmatic priorities contained in that plan?
7. Do you have a lengthy history that would indicate that your organization will still be around (and your mission still valid) for the next one hundred years?
8. Does the entire organization (board and staff) understand that an endowment does not replace (or take pressure off) annual fundraising but rather supplements funds raised annually?

9. Have you created proper policies, bylaws, and controls to protect your endowment principal from invasion?

If you answered no to most of these questions, you might still have some work to do before you are ready to undertake a successful endowment campaign.

It is important to remember that most organizations that have built large endowments have done so over a long period of time and through ongoing work, not just through a campaign. The largest endowments are usually built through working with donors in the areas of estate planning, where mega gifts to endowments are quite common. However, an endowment campaign is a great way to start an endowment fund and to bring visibility and awareness to your endowment needs and goals.

What is the best way to set a goal for endowment?

You have just completed a successful capital campaign, and you know that increasing the endowment will be one of your next priorities. How do you begin?

A good way for an institution to set a goal would be to have a goal for the total size of the endowment, to be achieved in a certain period of time. In other words, the endowment goal is both about raising funds and the management and growth of the endowment over time. One analysis is to look at endowments of peer institutions and try to set a total initial endowment goal, such as, "Our goal is to be in the top ten institutions by 2010." This could be a preliminary goal, and the formation of an endowment committee (or planned giving council) to monitor the total effort could solidify a more public goal after a year or two of work. Developing policies for endowment gifts, as well as professional assistance to deal with individual donor needs, is an important part of the process.

What is the recommended amount of endowment for a nonprofit? How do you articulate the need for endowment to a donor?

An organization's strategic plan should have three components: gift income, earned income, and endowment income. The amount of endowment would come from the results of the strategic plan's pro forma, which would show how much endowment is necessary for the organization to meet its long-term goal. In other words, there is no standard for size of endowment. The recommended amount of endowment that a nonprofit has can vary depending upon the nonprofit's strategic plan and specific use for endowment dollars. Some very elite nonprofit organizations have very large and significant endowments relative to their overall budgets.

They justify these large endowments by discussing the impact the endowments have on the excellence of their programs and research.

Other nonprofits identify their need for endowment based on their strategic plan and expected future growth. For example, if your current endowment provides 10 percent of your annual budget support, and you anticipate growing your budget by 50 percent over the next five years, then it could be reasonable to say you need to grow your endowment by 50 percent over the next five years as well.

Another method to justify and analyze the amount of endowment is to compare your endowment with similar nonprofits. This comparison can be used very effectively with prospective donors, especially those who might have had involvement with prestigious universities or museums whose quality and reputation are almost directly related to the size of their endowments.

Yet another part of the case for endowment is the funding of new programs that cannot be developed and sustained in any other manner. Ensuring that programs maintain a high quality is part of this, as is the opportunity to do new things.

So how do you make a case to a donor who thinks you don't need funds because you already have a reserve? Here are some options:

1. Discuss any programs that are desperately needed but have funding that might not continue. For example, if you have been funded with government grants for five years, but those grants will run out, talk about the need to endow the programs after the grants are over.
2. Discuss specific positions that are essential to the quality of programs and seek to endow those positions to ensure the excellence of programs in the future.
3. Show how your budget needs to increase to meet a growing demand.
4. Discuss the need to provide for the maintenance of physical facilities owned by the organization. For example, you might not need a new headquarters building today, but roofs might be very expensive tomorrow.
5. Show how an endowment for technology or another specific need can keep your organization effective and efficient.

In the end, how much endowment an organization can justify to its donors will depend on its long-range strategic plan and its ability to make a case for support for endowment.

Do you have a list of possible objections people might have to making an endowment gift, and appropriate responses?

One challenge they might pose is; "You only spend 5 percent of the income on my gift, can I invest and make more money and give it to you later?" A reply would be, "Yes we only spend 5 percent, but we invest the amount over this so that your fund can grow. Also, your gift to us grows tax free, and our organization can get the benefit of your gift working sooner." Or they might say, "I do not believe in endowment. The organization should pay its own way." To which you can respond, "While we cannot make you believe in endowment, we would point out that there have been few great institutions that have been built without a solid endowment." (You might ask them where they went to college and point out the endowment of that school.) "Without endowment we could not provide scholarships and assistance to the economically disadvantaged nor have a stable operation during tough economic times."

What standard wording is used to assure donors that their endowment gifts will be used for the purposes they were intended? Is there any form of contract?

Depending on the size and complexity of the gift there is usually some type of written donor agreement. This can be a letter that outlines the intent of the donor's use of the funds, the fact that he or she committed to the endowment of the organization, and the plan to manage those funds within the terms of other endowment funds. For example, a letter could state, "The $50,000 gift of Mr. and Mrs. Smith will be used as a permanent endowment fund, the income of which will be used to fund scholarships for students from Acme County, Iowa." It is a good idea to commit to giving the donors a yearly report on the performance of the endowment and an exact description of how the funds are being used. You might also want this agreement approved by your board of trustees or gift acceptance committee.

If the donor wants something more official, instead of writing the donor a letter, you can prepare the information as a written agreement and have both parties involved sign and witness the document. This way the donor has agreed to what you have written and has a signed document that the donor might view as legal. If this does not satisfy the donor, you might want your legal counsel to draft the document.

Where would I find guidelines for developing endowment spending policies?

The National Association of College and University Business Officers for several decades has conducted an annual survey of higher education endowment funds, including investment performance, investment policies, spending policies, and so on. More recently it has partnered with the National Association of Independent

Schools to conduct a similar survey. The results of the survey become available each April, and you can see how to get them at www.nacubo.org/accounting_finance/endowment_study. We believe that this is the most comprehensive and definitive resource available.

Typically, an endowment spending policy has two goals: (1) to grow the endowment to preserve its spending power against the effects of inflation and (2) to produce a steady stream of disposable income despite market fluctuations affecting investment results. One example of this is a spending policy allowing expenditure of 5 percent of a three-year average of the year-ending market value of the endowment.

How do we get documentation from donors that we are included in their will?

Someone wrote to us about a call he got from one of the organization's constituents. The donor had been in the organization's database for years but hadn't made any contribution other than purchasing two cookbooks in 1996. She mentioned in the phone call that she had remembered the organization in her will. They never received anything from her attorney confirming this. The writer was wondering where the organization stood legally in asking for documentation.

The important thing to keep in mind about a will is that it can be changed at any time a donor wishes to change it. So while they could ask her to send a note in writing about the will and tell them who has been named the executor, such a gesture does not guarantee that they will receive anything, because she could change the will later. The best thing to do is to strengthen the relationship with this individual, especially since she has not been a supporter or very active.

We wonder if the organization has any type of donor society that recognizes people who have included it in their wills. This can encourage people to leave the organization in their wills and to put a notice in writing.

Another approach is to arrange a meeting with this woman as a means of learning how she would like her estate assets to be used by the organization. Is there anything in particular that interests her? If so, maybe she would like to explore ways to give something now and still preserve her assets for her estate (through other planned giving vehicles such as charitable remainder trusts).

Starting a heritage society or founders society (or some other name that is appropriate to your organization) that recognizes people who have made planned gifts is a good way to encourage all donors to inform you if they have included you in their wills. Promoting the society on your website, in your newsletters, and in other printed materials will help encourage membership. You could even do a special mailing to targeted constituents who you think might be possible members. To be really effective, you will want some paperwork that the members complete to show that they are really eligible for membership. Have an annual event to recognize all new members in a given year. Be sure to also include lines on all pledge cards, business reply envelopes, and the like that donors can check if they would like more information about estate planning of if they have included your organization in their estate planning. Finally, when you conduct face-to-face cultivation, stewardship, or solicitation meetings with donors, tell them that you are starting the society and ask if they would be interested in membership.

How do I justify the need for a planned giving staff member to my board?

Now more than ever, development professionals are being asked to justify the money spent to raise money, especially when it comes to something that seems as difficult to measure as planned giving. Start by providing your board with general education about today's philanthropic world. Remember the estimate stated earlier in this chapter that $41 trillion will pass from one generation to the next between now and 2052. How your organization participates in the transfer will depend on your planned giving program. To learn more about this statistic and others that are similar, visit www.bc.edu/research/swri/features/wealth/.

Additionally, in the *Chronicle of Philanthropy*, Vince Stehle (1998, p. 30) noted,

[F]or years, fundraisers have anticipated a huge windfall from the "transfer of wealth" now underway as the parents of baby boomers die and dispose of their assets. But no one has come up with a good estimate for how much of the total transferred—which two Cornell University economists predict will be $10.4 trillion—charities can realistically expect to receive. Now, one researcher has presented a partial answer: nonprofit groups can count on getting about $1 trillion, "give or take a billion or two," he says, in the form of planned gifts—bequests and other donations that offer tax and other financial benefits that are more generous than those available for cash contributions.

A second message you need to communicate is that donors can give more if they are giving out of their assets and not just their income. If you do not have a planned giving program, you send the message to your donors that you only want gifts that are from their income. Also, many donors expect to have giving options. Remember, planned giving programs can help donors of all ages find the best method by which to make a large gift to your organization, not just find ways to get in the estates of older people.

Finally, look for ways to measure the impact of your planned giving program. Compile a list of all of the planned gifts, in all categories, that your organization is currently managing or expecting to receive. Update this list annually to show how it is growing. Using present value calculations, show your board how much money your organization will receive when these gifts mature.

What is your opinion on asking college students to purchase life insurance policies leaving the college as the beneficiary?

We have had experience with these kinds of plans before and generally think they are ineffective at creating positive results. First, they do not produce immediate income for your organization. Second, they often give the college student the impression that he or she has made a significant gift to the college and thus limit future giving as a result. Finally, these plans need to be seen for what they are: efforts to sell life insurance.

If you really want college students to feel tied to your college, start an annual giving program for them that is fun and exciting. Life insurance gifts might take many years to realize, and the cost of administration and premium payments can be time consuming and expensive.

Yet many organizations have policies in place that assure that the value of a life insurance gift outweighs the possible expense and liability. They do this by only accepting life insurance policies and commercial annuities as gifts when the organization is named as owner and beneficiary of 100 percent of the policy or contract. A life insurance policy on which the donor retains incidents of ownership, and on which the organization is only named beneficiary, is not a completed gift. This is an incomplete commitment, because the donor retains the right to change the beneficiary. If the policy is a paid-up policy, the value of the gift for the organization's gift accounting purposes is the policy's replacement cost, which is the cost to purchase an identical policy. If the policy is partially paid up, the value of the gift for the organization's gift accounting purposes is the policy's cash surrender value. (For IRS purposes, the donor's charitable income tax deduction is limited to the cash surrender value or the net premiums that have been paid on the policy, whichever is less.) Commercial annuities might or might not be appropriate for the donor to use as a gift because of complex tax issues. Donors should always consult financial advisors about the advisability or tax deductibility of these types of gifts.

These days should an organization new to planned giving accept a $25,000 gift annuity?

Short answer: probably. Long answer: 2002 and 2003 were challenging times for those administering charitable gift annuities because the return on institutional investments was at a low not seen in several decades. However, remember that the philosophy behind charitable gift annuities is that about 50 percent of the initial amount will eventually go to your institution. Thus current returns do not need to match the annuity amount going to the donor. This is why the American Council on Gift Annuities (ACGA) recommended new, lower rates beginning January 1, 2003. So the payout rates recommended by the ACGA www.acga-web.org) compared very favorably with rates currently being paid on certificates of deposits and fixed income securities. The rates are conservatively set. One of the rate-setting factors is a 6.5 percent expected investment return. The idea is that the charity will receive at least 50 percent of the original amount when the annuitants die.

When many older persons with investments in certificates of deposit experience dramatic declines in returns, charitable gift annuities can be a very attractive option for them. Charitable gift annuities are the second oldest form of planned gifts (after bequests) and a relatively easy gift option to add to a young planned giving program. Therefore it is worth exploring the acceptance of a $25,000 gift annuity (many established programs have a minimum of $100,000), and we recommend that you carefully research what is involved and adhere to the ACGA recommended rates. The ACGA website includes information on what requirements each state imposes on the issuance of charitable gift annuities, such as disclosure statements, minimum level of unrestricted assets available, state registration, and so on.

While some states do not require a reserve, some organizations establish one voluntarily for their own and the donors' comfort. You should give careful consideration to the stewardship issues of who will invest the funds and who will make the quarterly payments to the donors and provide them with the annual tax information.

Gift annuities are easy to administer, and the administration can be economically outsourced. If you have a planned giving program that has been emphasizing bequests, the issuance of gift annuities is the logical next step in the development of your program.

How should gifts of stock be handled?

Because giving an appreciated security is often a great way for a donor to make a larger gift and avoid capital gains, you want to have easy-to-follow policies and procedures for gifts of stock. Exhibit 10.1 presents some sample policies and procedures related to gifts of stock.

EXHIBIT 10.1.   SAMPLE STOCK ACCEPTANCE
POLICIES AND PROCEDURES.

Publicly Traded Securities

The organization may accept readily marketable securities, such as those traded on a stock exchange or the over-the-counter market. Such securities will be valued at the mean of the high and low quoted selling prices on the date the donor relinquished control of the assets in favor of the organization. For certain securities traded in the over-the-counter market, the mean of the bid and the "ask" is used to value the gift. It is the organization's policy to sell gifts of securities immediately. In accordance with standard gift reporting guidelines, neither losses nor gains realized on the sale of the stock by the organization, nor brokerage fees or other expenses associated with the transaction, will affect the valuation of the gift. If the number of shares involved is sufficient to be deemed by the organization's broker to have a potentially depressive impact on the price of the stock, the sale may be extended over a period of time necessary to avoid such an impact. If, in the opinion of the organization's investment advisors, the security is desirable and consistent with the organization's investment objectives, it may be held in the organization's endowment fund. Restricted stock subject to Securities and Exchange Commission Rule 144 shall be referred to the GAC. If accepted by the GAC, Rule 144 stock will be held until the restriction expires and then sold immediately. Gifts of bonds that require a holding period may be accepted and cashed when the holding period has expired. Gifts of securities will not be accepted under the following conditions:

- They are assessable or could create a liability for the organization or any of its entities.
- They are not assignable.
- On investigation, they have no apparent value.

Procedures

Our organization has established a brokerage account and instructions for donors on how to transfer stock to your account. Sample instructions to the donor are as follows:

> Thank you for your interest in supporting our organization with a gift of appreciated stock. In all cases of gifts of stock, one should notify the director of development or executive director before transfer of stock powers. Once the transfer has been approved, electronic delivery of your stock is the most efficient method of transfer. However, if you wish, you may also transfer certificates directly. To aid you in transferring a gift of stock, please use the following instructions.

Regardless of the method of transference, the donor or the broker must provide the following information:

- Donor's name and address
- Name and number of securities transferred
- Specific program, if any, to which you wish the gift directed

Please provide a letter, complete the gift form, or send an e-mail to indicate your intent to the director of development or executive director at [fax number and e-mail address].

Stock Transferred Electronically
The following will provide your broker with the necessary information to complete an electronic transfer of stock:

Organization's broker

Broker street address

City, state, zip

Phone number

Fax number

Agent bank number

DTC number

Account name

Organization name

Tax ID number

Account number

Securities Delivered by Mail
Send your unendorsed certificate(s) and a signed stock power form in separate envelopes by registered mail to

Director of development or executive director

Organization name

Address

City, state, zip

Summary

Planned giving should be an important part of every comprehensive development program for two important reasons. First, if it is a sustained effort, over a period of time it will produce results well beyond the investment in time and money. Second, it is very much in keeping with the growing tendency of donors to see contributions as investments. Planned giving strongly encourages donors to consider using not only income but also assets when making charitable gifts.

A simple beginning—asking donors to include your organization in their wills—is an activity virtually all organizations can undertake. We have worked with many organizations that tell us their best prospects for planned gifts are the donors who send $20 or so every few months for many years. While these donors often do not have much to give now, and their estates might not be much more than a few hundred thousand dollars, these types of gifts coming in on a regular basis can make a huge difference.

The sooner you begin, the sooner you will reap the rewards. Not only will your organization survive with planned gifts, for many it is the best strategy to thrive.

CHAPTER ELEVEN

FOUNDATION GRANTS: WRITING AND OTHER KEYS TO SUCCESS

Foundations exist to provide financial support to nonprofit organizations. Some foundations limit their support to specific nonprofits, while others choose to support organizations that fall within a certain interest area.

Because most foundations require a written request for funding, grant writing has become a profession. But you do not have to be a professional grant writer to secure funding from foundations.

In our experience, writing the grant is only a small part of the overall process of securing funding from a foundation, corporation, or other funding entity. The process also includes research, fact-finding, relationship building, and stewardship.

Many people new to grant writing want to create the perfect proposal that they can send to every foundation. This proposal is a myth. Every foundation should be treated as unique, because foundations do not make decisions—people do.

Get to know the people who are running the foundations, and you will be able to write many more winning grant proposals. In other words, by getting to know the decision makers, their interests, and their recommended format for grant requests, your grant writing will be successful.

This chapter will offer you additional ideas and strategies for approaching foundations and will answer the following questions:

- What are operating foundations? How are they different from other foundations?
- What is the best approach for securing funding from a community foundation?

- How do I find information on trusts?
- How should our organization tap into foundation support?
- What do *preselected, no unsolicited requests,* and *no applications* mean?
- What is the difference between a letter of inquiry and a proposal? What is the average length for each?
- What are the three most important things a foundation should read in my proposal?
- How much emotion should be in a proposal?
- Do I need to set justified margins in my proposals? Do I need to submit the proposal on special paper?
- A grant application asks for an audited financial statement, but we are eight months old and do not yet have one. How can we complete the application?
- Can I submit a request for the same item to more than one foundation?
- Is there a rule of thumb about how much more one can request in a formal proposal?
- We have applied to several foundations for grants in the past year. It is now time to submit another application for this year. Should our cover letter contain repeated information regarding our history and progress?
- How do I write a concept paper to initiate the grant application?
- Are you familiar with organizations that offer free grant-writing services to non-profits?
- Is it ethical to ask another organization for a copy of the grant proposal that they used to obtain a grant?
- A grants director called two days after a deadline to tell me that I had not followed the application guidelines. Did I blow it?
- How can I find volunteer grant proposal writers?
- Should I be using keywords as I ask for support?
- Will foundations fund transportation and food costs?

What are operating foundations? How are they different from other foundations?

Operating foundations fund only one organization. Foundations operated by state universities are the most common type of operating foundations. Virtually all state colleges and universities accept donations; however, the universities themselves are programs of the state government rather than 501(c)(3) organizations that can receive donations. The universities establish operating foundations that become registered charities and therefore can receive tax-deductible donations. Such operating foundations are also common in hospital settings.

To determine if a foundation is an operating foundation, look to Part III of its 990 form for its "Statement of Program Accomplishments." An operating foundation will explain its purpose with a phrase such as, "The University of [State] Foundation was chartered in 1947 to establish and maintain endowments for the support of academic programs at the University of [State]." The IRS Publication 578 defines the various kinds of private foundations and their tax requirements. This publication is available online at www.irs.gov/pub/irs-pdf/p578.pdf.

What is the best approach for securing funding from a community foundation?

Community foundations are typically collections of different funds that have been pooled to allow for better management and oversight than any one separate fund could have on its own. Funds at community foundations might be restricted (to an organization, group of organizations, or interest area), unrestricted, designated, or donor advised.

Before approaching a community foundation it is best to determine which funds would be most likely to support your organization. Look for funds that have supported organizations such as yours in the past. If a fund is donor advised, establishing a connection to the donor should be your first step.

Because they manage a variety of different funds, many community foundations maintain websites that explain the grant-making processes. The Foundation Center maintains a list of community foundations by state on its website at www.fdncenter.org/funders/grantmaker/gws_comm/comm.html.

How do I find information on trusts?

Trusts can be established for a variety of reasons. For example, a wealthy grandparent might set up a trust that helps to pay the living expenses of a grandchild. A charitable gift could come from such a trust if the trustee determined that a gift to the Boys & Girls Club fell within the guidelines of "living expenses" for the grandchild.

Because there are many kinds of trusts, and trusts are not obligated to file 990 forms with the IRS, information about them is usually difficult to obtain.

Charitable trusts are organizations that make donations but are typically set up as part of an estate plan. They operate much like charitable foundations but require less reporting. These might be permanent or temporary trusts. Typically, the decision makers for trust donations are the donors' lawyers, bankers, and other support professionals. While some trusts are created with very specific directions as to how and to whom donations can be made, others leave such decisions to the discretion of the trustees.

Getting to know the trust officers at your local banks and other financial institutions is a good first step toward identifying trusts that might be interested in funding your organization.

How should our organization tap into foundation support?

The first step is to research. Four sources for foundation research include the Foundation Center (www.fdncenter.org), Grantstation (www.grantstation.com), Guidestar (www.guidestar.org), and FundraisingINFO.com www.fundraisinginfo.com).

Research should help you identify the foundations that would be most interested in your organization. Questions to consider include the following:

- Does the foundation provide the type of support you are seeking? For example, if you need funding for a capital campaign, does the foundation provide capital funding?
- Does the foundation limit its funding to a specific geographic area? If so, are you in that area?
- What are the foundation's specific areas of interest? If this is not stated, look at the foundation's giving history. Has it previously supported programs and activities similar to yours?
- Is the foundation professionally staffed, or do the donors or board members manage it personally? Foundations that have staff generally want the staff to be involved in meeting with potential grant recipients to clarify the foundation's interests and to guide the potential recipients in the funding process. Family foundations, which are run by donors or board members, should be approached as individual donors. In other words, the best grant proposal in the world will not be nearly as important as involving and cultivating the foundation's board members.
- Does the foundation have published grant application procedures and guidelines?
- Who serves on the foundation board?
- What size grants does the foundation normally make? Are you seeking a grant within its normal range?

With your research complete, the next step is to identify the most direct path to arranging a meeting with a board member or with the appropriate foundation representative. If a face-to-face meeting is not possible, schedule a telephone call to discuss your program with them. This is a great activity in which to involve your board members and development committee. Ask for their assistance in scheduling meetings with foundation representatives that they know.

In the meeting, ask about the foundation's goals, objectives, and guidelines for funding. Then follow their advice and guidelines to a T! In other words, build relationships with the staff and board members of the foundations first, and then write the grant. You will have much more success.

What do *preselected, no unsolicited requests,* and *no applications* mean?

Sometimes *preselected* really means that there are only a few organizations that the foundation can legally support because of the way it is incorporated. Other times, it means that the foundation will not accept proposals because its board decides which programs it wants to support based on their involvement with organizations, not on applications.

No unsolicited requests might also mean that they invite certain groups to apply and that you should not apply if you are not invited to apply. In this case, submitting a proposal without some type of personal contact might be a completely worthless activity.

Foundations that give to preselected organizations typically give to organizations in which their original donors and board members have an interest and involvement. To become a preselected organization, you can follow these steps:

1. Research the foundation to determine who makes the grant decisions. Does the foundation have a board? Who is on the board?
2. Look at the kinds of programs they have funded in the past.
3. Ask your board members and other fundraising volunteers to review the list of foundation board members to see if they have any personal connections with them.
4. If you find a connection, ask your board member to contact the foundation board member and say, "I am on the board of [name of your organization], and we are interested in learning more about your foundation. Can you spend a half hour with [your executive director] and me next week to tell us more about how we could become a funding option for your foundation?
5. At this point, a few things might happen: the foundation board member will say yes and meet with you. The foundation board member will say, "We have a staff person who handles all of that; you really need to call that person." In this case, your board member should call the suggested staff person and say, "I was talking with [name of foundation board member], who suggested that I call you. I am on the board of [organization], and we are interested in learning more about your foundation. Can you spend a half hour with [name of

staff person] and me?" Or the foundation board member might say, "We have already made our decision for this year" or "We only give to certain organizations." In which case, your board member should be trained to say, "That's okay. We would still like to meet with you to learn more about the foundation."

6. When you get to your meetings, be prepared to listen and learn about the foundation and what they like to see in a grant request. Also be prepared to discuss your programs and projects that might interest the foundation. Before completing the meeting, be sure to ask, "Would you suggest that we apply for a grant? What would be the best way for us to apply for a grant? Do you like to fund projects in full? Would a request for [dollar amount] for our [program name] be in line with your current funding priorities?"

Another approach is to identify the board members of these foundations and again try to find your own board members and volunteers who have connections with them. Then seek to involve the foundation board members in an activity, tour of your facility, or some other event. Use this first connection to involve the person who makes the decision. Once that person is involved, and you have an established relationship, ask about the foundation.

What is the difference between a letter of inquiry and a proposal? What is the average length for each?

A *letter of inquiry* is usually two to three pages and is sent to request information about how to apply for a grant. A *proposal* can be two pages or twenty pages, depending upon the requirements of the foundation. In general, we do not favor sending letters of inquiry unless the foundation clearly states that it wishes to be contacted in this manner.

In our experience, unless the foundation requires letters of inquiry, many foundations either ignore letters of inquiry or send a rejection letter before you even have a chance to present your case.

What are the three most important things a foundation should read in my proposal?

The three most important points a foundation needs to hear from you are these:

1. By funding you, the foundation will accomplish one or more of its stated objectives and goals.
2. You are capable of doing what you say you will do with the funding.
3. You know how much the program will cost and how you will fund it (especially if you are only asking the foundation for a portion of the costs).

The three most important things are also the things that the foundation says are important. Read the guidelines carefully, talk with them, see what really interests them, and include these things in your proposals. Some foundations want a lot of facts and figures and information on how you will report to them. Others, typically smaller family foundations, just want to know that they will be making a good investment in the community.

How much emotion should be in a proposal?

The level of emotion will be determined by the foundation. If it is a staff-run foundation, you are probably better off sticking to the facts and figures, which can be very heartfelt. That is, if an organization is helping more youth for fewer dollars and can prove it with facts and figures, the proposal will probably win out over one that is full of emotion by an organization whose programs do not reach nearly as many kids for the same money.

Do I need to set justified margins in my proposals? Do I need to submit the proposal on special paper?

There is no need for justified margins, unless the person receiving the proposal says that is how they want the proposal formatted. Same with the kind of paper you use; unless it is specified in the grant guidelines, use whatever you have that is better than copy paper.

A grant application asks for an audited financial statement, but we are eight months old and do not yet have one. How can we complete the application?

Make sure you have good financial records. Be prepared to show the foundation everything, from monthly income statements to your checking account register.

Have your board pass a resolution that commits the organization to an annual audit. Ask your board treasurer or finance chair to secure a firm to do the audit pro bono. This way you can include a copy of the resolution in your grant request.

Contact the foundation and ask the appropriate program or grant officer how you should present your financial information in light of your organization's age. This gives you a great opportunity to discuss your project a little bit (if you have not already done so) and get some feedback directly from the foundation on the proper approach.

Can I submit a request for the same item to more than one foundation?

When submitting grant applications, I have generally tried to submit grants only for the actual dollars needed. I felt I would be "double-dipping" if I made several requests for the same item. However, if a grant recipient does not approve the grant application, then I do not have all the money I need.

If you have a good relationship with the foundations—that is, you are actually sending requests to foundations that you have talked and met with—then you should request the full amount needed for a project, unless the foundation has advised you to do otherwise. If you get a grant for the full amount needed and you have other requests outstanding for the same project, you can call the other foundations, make them aware that the project has been funded, and ask if you might resubmit a request for a different project.

Is there a rule of thumb about how much more one can request in a formal proposal?

We have a rule of thumb that if you are applying to a foundation for the first time, you should look at their past grants and apply for an amount that is within the smaller end of their dollar range. So if they have made grants of $5,000, $10,000, and $25,000 in the last few years, as a new applicant you would apply for $5,000.

Of course, this does not take into account the guidance and advice the foundation has provided in the application process. What you request should have more to do with what the foundation tells you than rules of thumb.

We suggest that in all cases you ask the foundation, "Would it be appropriate for us to request a grant of [dollar amount] for this project?"

One of our clients sent an informal letter to a foundation that explained their program and included a budget. The foundation liked the idea and asked the organization to send a formal proposal. In finalizing the request, the organization wanted to add some new components that would raise the original budgeted and requested amount.

In a case such as this, having a conversation is essential. Here are two possible approaches:

1. Call the foundation and talk with someone about these new components. Be up-front with them about the fact that when you first submitted the budget you had not fully explored the full nature of what was needed to run the program. If the new components are essential to the program's success, explain why. Then ask if the foundation would accept a proposal for the full amount of the budget. If the new components are nice-to-have, nonessential items, be

up-front about that too and ask if it would be okay to include them in the formal proposal request.

2. Include the new components in the total budget for your formal proposal but clearly show how you need to seek other funding sources for the new components. This is very important to do if you think the new components are essential to the program. The last thing you want to do is get funding from this foundation and then not be able to fully implement the program.

We have submitted applications to several foundations for grants in the past year. It is now time to submit another application for this year. Should our cover letter contain repeated information regarding our history and progress?

As long as you have maintained the relationship with the foundation board and staff, we think that it would be acceptable to send another cover letter with similar points from the first letter. Make sure that you make reference to your previous letter or grant request. Any progress reports or updates should be new information and not repeated from last year. Some foundations receive hundreds of requests a month, so do not assume that the foundation recalls all of the information you have sent in the past.

To make the biggest impact with the foundation, you should request a personal appointment with a foundation representative. This appointment would give you a wonderful opportunity to make your case and personally present your organization's mission face to face. Remember, people give to people. If you do not know the foundation representative, you should ask your board members if they could be helpful in securing the appointment.

How do I write a concept paper to initiate the grant application?

Concept papers are usually internal documents written to develop institutional support for a grant concept or new program or project.

If you are considering using a concept paper in-house to develop institutional support, prior to seeking outside funding, we recommend that the paper be no longer than a few pages. Involve all of your organization's key decision makers in the review of the concept. In addition to the paper, be sure to include information on possible funders and clear next steps.

If you are developing this for a potential funder, again we recommend that you do not initiate a grant process in this manner unless the foundation clearly specifies this as its application process. If it says this is the process, then ask if the foundation has guidelines for a concept paper's format.

Otherwise, we strongly recommend that you (or another member of your organization's leadership) contact the appropriate people at the foundation and ask to meet with them to discuss your organization's mission and programs. This meeting should be used to discuss various concepts and get feedback on them.

Are you familiar with organizations that offer free grant-writing services to nonprofits?

We get nervous when we hear that something is free. Why? Because at the end of the day, everyone has bills to pay, and if they are not making their money from the work they do for you, they have to be making it somewhere and somehow. Review these kinds of offers very carefully. We suggest that you even ask someone at the company offering the free service exactly how they make money. If it is a for-profit company, it will not stay in business very long doing work for free. Listen to the response. If it is hard to understand, then it is probably designed to hide something. Also look carefully at the people behind the company. Do they have experience with grant writing? Do they have experience working with nonprofits? Do they plan on keeping a percentage of the dollars raised? Or, are they tying this service to some other aspect of their services? Get answers to these questions and be sure to get a list of clients served. Call those clients and ask about their satisfaction with the free service.

Is it ethical to ask another organization for a copy of the grant proposal that they used to obtain a grant?

Sure, there is nothing unethical about asking. Just remember to establish your own relationship with the foundation—go see them or talk with the foundation before submitting your own proposal. The foundation's funding priorities might have changed since it funded the other organization.

A grants director called two days after a deadline to tell me that I had not followed the application guidelines. Did I blow it?

You mailed a grant request on November 30 to meet a December 15 deadline. You knew when you were looking at the grant guidelines that the information was not complete. You called the foundation to confirm that you had all the grant guidelines and application pages. The foundation grants director assured you that you had everything you needed. The grants director called two days after the deadline leaving a message that you had not followed their grant guidelines and that you could contact her on December 30. The last and most important page of the grant guidelines was not in the copies you received from the foundation. What now?

Here is a case where it is so important to do as you are told. The grants director said to contact her on December 30, so you need to contact her on December 30. When you call her, ask if you can send the additional information and still be considered for this deadline. If she is hesitant to allow you to do so, promise to get it in within 24 hours (be sure that you are ready to do that). If she still is hesitant, explain what happened, without placing blame on anyone, and ask her to reconsider. If that does not work, ask her if she thinks it would be appropriate for you to apply in the next funding cycle. Be sure to find out about the next deadline and all of the guidelines.

No matter what happens, use this as a way to build your relationship with the grants director. Keep a really positive attitude when you call and look for opportunities to learn more about the foundation and share your mission. Make the grants director your ally, and you will have a better chance of getting funding either now or in the future.

How can I find volunteer grant proposal writers?

One way to find a volunteer grant writer is to go to www.volunteermatch.org. There you will be able to post your need for a volunteer grant writer to people who are looking for volunteer opportunities. Another suggestion is to contact local colleges and universities in your area to find out if they have degrees in nonprofit management. If they do, ask about getting a student intern.

One final suggestion is to "grow your own." Find a volunteer who feels passionately about your organization and ask that person to help you write grants. If your volunteer writes well and follows directions, then you have a volunteer grant writer. Keep in mind that the secrets to writing a successful grant request are establishing relationships with the decision makers at the foundation, meeting with them, listening to what they say about your project, and following their instructions for submitting a request.

Should I be using keywords as I ask for support?

Keywords are words we use to help define and refine searches. More often than not, they are not created by the foundations but by the research service—the company that is maintaining the information about that foundation. Keywords are not necessarily terms used in proposals. But again, you should try and meet with the foundation to hear its terminology so that you can use it in your proposal. A great place to find a foundation's keywords is in its annual report, if it publishes one.

Will foundations fund transportation and food costs?

Let's say you hire two buses to transport your clients (youth ages seven to thirteen) between their homes and your program and to and from field trips. You see a lot of hungry children in your program and would love to help them get at least one decent meal each day. Will foundations fund these expenses?

If you have a relationship with a foundation that is not prohibited from funding such things, and you can personally present your case to a person related to the foundation (staff or board member), then there should be no reason why a foundation would not fund such things. Additionally, when it comes to feeding children (or adults for that matter), be sure to check out government-related programs. A helpful resource for finding government-related grants is www.grants.gov.

Summary

In concluding this chapter, we have one last piece of advice on how to give your foundation grant writing an even greater competitive advantage. Once you have received funding, keep the foundation informed regarding your use of the funds. Many foundation representatives have told us that they find it difficult to get feedback from their grant recipients on the use and impact of the grants. Stand out from the crowd. If the foundation requires reports on its grants, get yours in on time.

Even if the foundation does not require reports, send them anyway. Better yet, go meet with the foundation representative who helped you get the grant and update him or her on your progress, or invite foundation staff to visit and see the impact of the grant firsthand. This will go a long way toward building your relationship with the foundation and keep you from becoming just another one of "those nonprofits we only hear from when they need money."

CHAPTER TWELVE

CORPORATE DOLLARS: SPONSORSHIP, MARKETING, AND MORE

Corporate giving has consistently been the smallest segment of all giving in the United States. In fact, results from *Giving USA*'s annual reports on philanthropy usually show corporate giving making up roughly 5 percent of all charitable dollars. Often when we do fundraising workshops we will start with a basic overview about the fact that individuals are responsible for such a high percentage of the charitable dollars that are given away each year. Usually our workshop participants are surprised at the small percentage of giving from those big corporations.

It would seem that many people involved in fundraising would know that corporate giving represents a small portion of the charitable landscape. Yet corporations tend to consume the thoughts of many fundraising volunteers and staff when it is time to talk about large gifts, new prospects, or potential major donors. During capital campaigns, we usually hear at least one board member or fundraising volunteer ask, "What about the big corporations? When do we go after them?" Or as someone else has said, "We need to have a strategy for those big national corporations. They could make a large gift and not even miss it." We have even known nonprofits to hire certain consultants or staff members in order to go after the big corporate money.

Because this way of thinking is so prevalent and because most companies want a good rate of return on their charitable dollars, raising money from corporations has become a highly competitive area of fundraising.

This chapter will prepare you for the competition by explaining the ways that corporations invest their philanthropic dollars. This chapter will also answer the following questions:

- What do I need to know to successfully increase the corporate support of my organization?
- What are the different ways a corporation can provide support?
- What steps should we take to solicit in-kind gifts?.
- How do you find out if a company has a matching gift program? How does an organization become eligible to receive matching gifts?
- What are tax credits and what relationship do they have to corporate fundraising?
- How can I research larger corporations and their giving?
- What should be in a letter to past corporate event sponsors if their last gifts were ten years ago and your contacts are no longer there?
- Should we consider having different sponsorship opportunities for local and national companies or for larger and smaller ones?
- Does it increase our likelihood of getting funding from a corporation if one of its employees is on our board?
- Our original contact at a large company promised to help us receive a grant. She is no longer with the company, and now our grant is lost. Should we ask the ex-employee to assist us?
- We sent over one hundred letters to suppliers we have used for over twenty-seven years. In the six weeks since the mailing, we have received one return of $100. What should we do?
- My boss wants me to send letters to all the chamber of commerce members in our town. I think that personal contacts would be more effective and would like to involve our fundraising committee to assist with these contacts. He says no. What should I do?
- Do you have any suggestions for accountability standards for our corporate grant writer position?

What do I need to know to successfully increase the corporate support of my organization?

Here are some basics to keep in mind when approaching corporations. First, do your homework. Know what the company does to make money. There is nothing more frustrating to a company than to be asked by a solicitor, "What does your company do?" Companies will want to know if your proposal will help it acquire or maintain its customer base. So know who its customers are. Find out what its ownership structure is. Is it a privately held or publicly traded company? Privately held companies will make decisions based on the owner's interests much more than a publicly traded company will. Most importantly, research the corporation's history of giving. The history of other philanthropic giving, not simply the size of the business, will be your important research fact in determining the likelihood of support.

Second, remember that corporations do not decide where to give money. People at corporations make these decisions. Identifying who makes the funding decisions is an important step. Start your cultivation with the person as high on the corporate ladder as you can access. This applies even if the corporation has a grant manager. If you have a board member who knows the CEO, start with the CEO. Worst case, the CEO will refer you to the grant manager, who will know that the CEO sent you.

Third, follow up on everything. Corporations put their money where they believe they will get the best results. If you meet deadlines, send materials that are requested in a timely fashion, or take their advice, you send the message that your organization is organized, well managed, and able to produce results.

Fourth, be patient yet persistent. Some corporations take a long time to make decisions. If you are seeking a large corporate gift, be prepared to answer questions and to discuss different ideas with different decision makers. This is especially true if the corporation has a staff that is solely dedicated to making grants.

Fifth, clearly show the corporate prospect how this investment in your organization will make a positive impact on their customers, their employees, their community, and, most importantly, their financial goals and corporate objectives.

Finally, say thank you for everything. The manner in which you acknowledge corporate gifts is just one more way to create a competitive advantage.

What are the different ways a corporation can provide support?

Corporations can support nonprofit organizations in a variety of ways. These include the following:

1. Gifts in kind: materials, products, or other resources
2. Sponsorships of events and activities
3. Cash gifts and grants
4. Gifts that match the gifts of its employees, board members, or former employees and board members
5. Cause-related marketing efforts (in which the company commits to give a percentage of its sales of certain products or services)

What steps should we take to solicit in-kind gifts?

Before soliciting or accepting in-kind gifts, make sure you have a complete list of what is really needed. The list should correspond with your organization's needs and your ability to store excess materials. Also, set standards of what kind of materials you will and will not accept. Draft a set of standards and ask your board development committee to review them for board approval. This is an important step because you do not want to collect and dispose of junk or have to explain to a donor why your organization will not accept something.

Make a list of possible corporate donors and review them with your development committee to identify your best prospects for in-kind contributions. Try to get a board member or volunteer to lead the effort to contact as many of the possible donors in person as possible.

Help volunteers make personal contact by sending a letter in advance (such as the one that appears in Exhibit 12.1).

Make sure every volunteer has the list of needed materials before making a visit. Solicit the companies in a sequential order based on who might give you the most materials. For example, if you are looking for building products, go to the company that has the ability to donate all the lumber you need. Ask them to do so; if they cannot, then go on to other possible smaller donors. This will reduce the risk of getting too much and then having storage problems.

EXHIBIT 12.1.   SAMPLE IN-KIND GIFT SOLICITATION LETTER.

Dear [name],

Last year more than three hundred community residents joined together to help the [name] family realize the dream of home ownership. Through our program, companies such as [names], churches, and organizations donated time, materials, and money to make this happen.

Now the [name] family is paying back this generosity to help other families attain the same dream.

You can help by donating [items]. We have an exciting corporate program that will promote your company's involvement, provide a team-building opportunity for your employees, and [other benefits].

I would like to meet with you soon to tell you more about our corporate program and will call to arrange a convenient time for us to meet.

Sincerely,

[your name here]

Use any gift in kind as an opportunity to show a corporation that your organization uses gifts wisely and is very appreciative of its donors.

How do you find out if a company has a matching gift program? How does an organization become eligible to receive matching gifts?

According to the Council for Advancement and Support of Education (www.case.org), as of May 2005 there were over eighty-six hundred matching gift programs in the United States. These include programs that had some form of a matching grants program that either matched employees' gifts or made grants in conjunction with employees' volunteer time.

The rules that companies follow for matching grants change all the time. Sometimes it is easier to ask your individual donors if their companies match gifts than to keep up with all the changes. To facilitate this strategy, organizations can send their supporters information on how to contact their employer to find out if they have a matching grant program. Sample language for such a note follows in Exhibit 12.2.

Another approach is to include a line on reply cards and pledge cards that reads, "Will your employer match this gift?"

Finally, the most complete list available is through CASE. They sell either the list or special brochures you can use with your annual fund. (CASE members receive a discount.)

You can contact CASE through their website (www.case.org—go to the "Matching Gift Clearinghouse" button). Or you can call them at 202-328-2273.

What are tax credits and what relationship do they have to corporate fundraising?

Loosely defined, *tax deductions* reduce a corporation's income, while *tax credits* reduce a corporation's actual income tax. In other words, tax credits are applied to reduce the amount of taxes owed. (Table 12.1 provides an example.)

EXHIBIT 12.2.   SAMPLE MATCHING GIFT APPEAL.

More than eight thousand companies match the contributions of their employees. If your company has a matching gifts program, you could increase your support to our organization by two or three times your gift. Please contact your benefits manager or human resource director to determine if your company will match your gifts to our organization. Share with your company that we are a 501(c)(3) organization dedicated to [brief description of organization's mission].

TABLE 12.1.   TAX CREDIT ILLUSTRATION.

The following figures assume a 20 percent corporate tax rate.

	Illustration of Tax Deduction	Illustration of Tax Credit
Sales	$1,000,000	$1,000,000
Expenses	$750,000	$750,000
Charitable contributions not eligible for tax credit	$100,000	$75,000
Gross profit	$150,000	$175,000
Taxes owed	$30,000	$35,000
Minus tax credit	—	$25,000
Net taxes owed	$30,000	$10,000

In the United States, some states have laws that allow corporations to reduce the amount of state taxes they have to pay by making charitable contributions to qualified nonprofit organizations. For example, during 2002, eleven states—Connecticut, Delaware, Florida, Indiana, Kansas, Maryland, Missouri, Nebraska, Pennsylvania, Virginia, and West Virginia—had neighborhood assistance programs (NAPs) that provided tax credits to businesses that contributed (cash, materials, or staff) to community-based nonprofit organizations, often targeting low-income people and communities.

We have also seen programs that provide tax credits for contributions made to educational organizations or childcare agencies. These types of programs make it very attractive for corporations to give to nonprofits that qualify. Contact your local government representative to find out about its tax credit programs.

How can I research larger corporations and their giving?

Many public companies publish information on their philanthropy and community programs on their websites. If they have a corporate foundation, start by researching information about it. Remember some corporations give from both their foundations and other budgets.

Company websites also usually have a list of their officers and directors. So acquiring good supersearch skills using an Internet search engine can often provide you with free access to much of what you need to research a corporation.

Most international businesses still focus grants in areas where they have local operations. Before you spend a lot of time researching companies, preparing proposals, and so on, it is a good idea to contact the local operations of these larger companies and involve their staff in assisting you in getting support from the national office. One reason for this is that some companies require that the local store or office support all requests.

What should be in a letter to past corporate event sponsors if their last gifts were ten years ago and your contacts are no longer there?

Because it has been ten years, it would be better to treat these corporate contributors more like new prospects. This means rebuilding the relationship and making personal visits. In other words, letters might not be adequate tools for this task, though a letter could be used to open the door to a meeting. With this in mind, the letter might say something such as "[Name of company] has been a valued supporter of our organization, and we are interested in discussing how we can, once again, form a mutually beneficial relationship. I will call you next week to schedule a convenient time for us to meet."

Should we consider having different sponsorship opportunities for local and national companies or for larger and smaller ones?

Yes. This is particularly important if you have a history of support from local, smaller organizations and you now want to have higher-priced sponsorship opportunities without losing the local relationships. This was the challenge one of our clients was facing when they wrote to us.

Fortunately, they were riding a bit of a wave of interested corporate sponsors. In response, they raised their sponsorships level to a minimum of $10,000. This new level was too high for some of their long-term local corporate sponsors to reach. As a result, the organization was scrambling to find ways to maintain these local contacts.

In our experience, it is a good idea to place a high value on long-term local corporate support. Local companies can help in many ways. They can open doors to other potential supporters in the community. Their employees can become volunteers. And there is a chance they will become larger companies or get bought out by larger companies and be able to make or influence larger gifts.

Thus we find it is helpful to create sponsorships at a variety of amounts so that all above a certain level can participate. Or tie some sponsorship opportunities directly to local activities and events and try to make them most affordable and attractive to local businesses.

Does it increase our likelihood of getting funding from a corporation if one of its employees is on our board?

It should help. Corporations generally like to give where their employees are involved. The position your board member holds in the company will determine whether he or she is the best person to solicit the corporation.

Be wary of recruiting people to your board just as corporate representatives. Whether they can influence the giving of their companies or not, you want each board member to fulfill the basic responsibilities of personal giving and participation in other board duties.

Our original contact at a large company promised to help us receive a grant. She is no longer with the company, and now our grant is lost. Should we ask the ex-employee to assist us?

We hear stories like this on a regular basis. Corporate restructuring, layoffs, and pressure to meet quarterly numbers for Wall Street are just a few of the things that can interfere with a nonprofit's relationship with a corporation.

One of our clients recently requested a large donation from one of their suppliers at the suggestion of the head of their marketing department. The head of the marketing department suggested a gift of $50,000 was possible because their CEO was very interested in the nonprofit's programs.

The marketing head was really excited and had great ideas. Our client sent the marketing head all the material she requested. Then one month went by with no response. Our client called her, and she explained that her position had changed and that she would be working as a consultant from her home. As a result, someone else would be in charge of their giving, but the marketing head promised to brief the new person fully.

When our client called, the new giving manager knew nothing about the nonprofit or the promised $50,000, and he said, "We cannot give to your nonprofit because we only give to one charity, and they just had their big fundraiser."

While these types of situations can be frustrating, you cannot afford to get discouraged or angry every time there is a glitch in the road. If you do, you might never get to a big gift.

When these sorts of things happen, the number-one rule to keep in mind is, "Don't burn any bridges." The marketing department head was doing her job when it was her job. It is no longer her job. The new person might be overwhelmed with responsibilities, and it might have been easier for him to say, "We only give to one charity."

In such a situation, it is a good idea to send a "thank you for taking the time to speak with me" note to the new staff person and to include a small bit of information about your organization. Then call the former marketing head, since she is still a consultant. (We would not recommend this if she were now working for a different company or had left the company completely.) Tell her that things did not go well with the new person. Ask for her advice on what to do next. If she does not have any ideas on this, thank her for her time and for all she did to help. Then continue your cultivation relationship with the new marketing person and start working your network of board members and others to see if anyone knows the CEO personally and can get you a one-on-one meeting with him. Perseverance is needed in corporate fundraising, even if you have had a request denied.

We sent over one hundred letters to suppliers we have used for over twenty-seven years. In the six weeks since the mailing, we have received one return of $100. What should we do?

We received a letter from some employees of an organization who formed a nonprofit arm of their for-profit company. They sent over one hundred letters to suppliers they have used for over twenty-seven years. In the six weeks following the mailing, they received one return of $100. Their boss is furious because the company spent millions with some of those suppliers.

In a situation such as this, there are two issues to address: one is how to raise additional dollars from suppliers, and the other is managing the boss. We suggested that they will raise the most money by following up by phone. When they call, they should talk to the person as high up in the company as they can reach. Schedule as many face-to-face visits as they can. Tell them that the purpose of the visit is to tell them more about the nonprofit's mission. In the meeting, tell them about the organization's mission and clients. Then they should explain that they are contacting suppliers and others who have had long-standing relationships with the for-profit company. They should ask the supplier to join a founders' circle or some other gift club. Make the membership to the founders' circle equal to $1,000 a year or whatever is appropriate.

In the meantime, they should talk with their boss and explain that the letters were the first step in their strategy for contacting the suppliers; now they need his help to move to get face-to-face meetings. They should explain to the boss that corporate giving only makes up about 5 percent of total giving and that vendors are generally not the best source of philanthropic funds for most organizations, especially if they are not used to making contributions.

My boss wants me to send letters to all the chamber of commerce members in our town. I think that personal contacts would be more effective, and would like to involve our fundraising committee to assist with these contacts. He says no. What should I do?

Most organizations have some group of volunteers that help solicit corporate sponsors. If your boss does not want you to access the fundraising committee's help with this, ask if you might put together a different group of volunteers. Have a suggested list with you and a plan showing what they will do.

However, it seems that your boss has a different understanding of your job than you do. If these are true sponsorships (having real marketing value to the corporate donor), then you can rely less on volunteers. But if the funds you are seeking are actually gifts, then you will serve best by engaging others to help you. Consider having this type of conversation with your boss so that you can develop the right strategy for your particular situation.

Do you have any suggestions for accountability standards for our corporate grant writer position?

The first step toward establishing these types of standards is to review your history. How many grants has your organization gotten in the past? From how many companies? Who solicited these grants? Who wrote them—a full-time person or a part-time person? If a part-time staff person wrote them, and now you will have a full-time person, you can use the part-time achievements to guide your goal setting.

If you have not had anyone in this position, you also need to take into account the following:

- Does your organization already have a written case for support that clearly shows the funding needs and priorities? If so, this will cut down considerably on the grant writer's need to gather information and get internal support to write grants. If you do not have such a document, the grant writer, with your assistance, will need to spend three to four months just identifying funding priorities for the organization, gathering data to support those priorities, and then researching potential funders.
- Will organizational leadership personally help present grant proposals to corporations? Or will the grant writer be on his or her own in submitting proposals? Making personal presentations greatly increases the success rate of grants—sometimes increasing a close ratio from 10 percent to 80 or even 90 percent.
- What tools will you provide to the grant writer to do research? With access to commercial services, a lot of research can be done in a short time because they are available online twenty-four hours a day, seven days a week. Without these types of tools, research will take longer.

Finally, we caution against establishing a standard for number of grants written. Too many people can generate hundreds of boilerplate proposals to meet that kind of standard. Instead, try establishing standards for the following:

- Number of new possible corporate grant sources identified
- Number of grant sources qualified by research
- Number of corporate grant sources contacted for initial meetings
- Number of initial meetings held with potential granters
- Number of proposals written in follow-up to initial meetings
- Number of proposals funded
- Total dollars raised

Summary

As you have read in this chapter, corporate giving can be tricky business. There is simply not a large pool of money waiting for you. Corporate giving, like other types of effective fundraising, is based on a solid case and personal relationships. Also, remember that there is a major difference between giving by large, publicly traded companies and private companies. Given a choice, you should focus on privately held companies whose leadership has some involvement or connection with your organization and much more flexibility in their giving.

CHAPTER THIRTEEN

TECHNOLOGY: EMBRACE IT

Technology has had a close relationship with fundraising for many years. The invention of the telephone made telemarketing possible. Typewriters and copy machines allowed for the production of mass-produced letters. Word processing programs made it even easier to produce large numbers of letters, all of which were personally addressed instead of using *Dear Friend* or another such phrase in the salutation. Television and radio have played their parts as well. Databases and database programs that can store large quantities of data have increased the constituency potential for many nonprofits.

In the past decade, the personal computer and the Internet have made technology's impact on fundraising even greater. Consider that Howard Dean's U.S. presidential campaign in 2003 raised $3.6 million online in three months through e-mail and web-based solicitations (www.directmag.com, 2003). And in the aftermath of the December 2004 tsunami, *USA Today* (Iwata, 2005) reported that more than $350 million was raised online in less than a month.

With a computer, Internet access, and an e-mail program even the smallest nonprofits with small budgets can communicate electronically with potential supporters without the expense of direct mail (assuming they know how to collect permission-based e-mail addresses). Research by Harvard Business School predicts that nearly one-third of all dollars will be contributed online by as early as 2010, because donors are becoming more comfortable with this method of giving, and many donors actually prefer it (Legace, 2005).

As a result, technological competency has become a necessary job skill for most nonprofit professionals. We find few fundraising jobs that do not require some computer knowledge or expertise. In fact, we would venture to say that comfort with e-mail programs, word processing programs, spreadsheets, and presentation software are necessary skills for all fundraising professionals.

Yet for many fundraising professionals technology is still a bit scary. It seems that fear keeps many from embracing technology in a way that could benefit their organizations.

This chapter should help you see that you are not alone in your technology struggles. It will also demystify things such as fundraising software, e-mail campaigns, websites, and more technology issues while answering the following questions:

- What impact can technology have on a fundraising program?
- How do I convince my board and staff that we need to invest in and use proven organizational tools for our fundraising efforts?
- What steps should we take before purchasing a fundraising software system?
- What are some pitfalls I should avoid when making a decision about fundraising software?
- What are some innovative ways that nonprofits are using technology?
- How do I convince my board to invest in a website?
- Should we sell our list of e-mail addresses to generate revenue?
- What are the laws that impact Internet-based fundraising efforts?
- Can you really raise more money via e-mail than you can via direct mail?
- Does every nonprofit need a website?
- What are some key elements of a good nonprofit website?
- What are the advantages of an e-newsletter, and how do we start one?

What impact can technology have on a fundraising program?

Technology can determine a fundraising program's level of competitiveness and its ability to sustain growth. The adequacy of an organization's technology can determine many factors:

- The number of donors and prospects with whom it can maintain personalized correspondence
- The speed with which it can issue thank you letters to donors
- The number of volunteers it can engage in activities
- The amount of information it can manage regarding donors and prospects
- The cost to process a gift (which affects return on dollars invested in fundraising)

- The speed with which it can produce timely fundraising campaigns and appeals
- The ease with which it can analyze fundraising programs and their effectiveness and provide this information to supporters and the public

How do I convince my board and staff that we need to invest in and use proven organizational tools for our fundraising efforts?

Start by making a list of the negatives of multiple databases: duplication of information, need to update information in multiple places to maintain records, increased staff time spent entering data in multiple places, need to extract data from multiple locations to produce reports on the fundraising program's costs and revenues, increased risk of losing important historical data, and others. You can further make your case by supplementing this list with specific examples of these time-consuming tasks and by sharing the following thoughts.

Suppose that you receive a call from a donor who has decided that she wants to make a substantial gift to your organization. While on the phone with this person, you look up her record in the database that you maintain. In it, you see that she has funded a particular program. So you begin to discuss that program. The donor then asks what the program's financial needs are, and you mention that they have a capital budget of $5,000 for the next year. The donor says that sounds good and that you will receive a check within the next couple of weeks.

After you hang up the phone, you proudly tell your co-workers about the gift you have secured. Before you finish your story, however, your executive director becomes angry because she had been talking to this donor for months about another program area that has even greater funding needs, and this information had been recorded in her contact database. If you had a comprehensive database you would have known all of these interests and could, perhaps, have suggested a more substantial funding opportunity in that other area or at least have known to transfer the donor's call to your executive director.

Or suppose that your supervisor or a board member calls and is having lunch with a donor in twenty minutes (not an uncommon occurrence) and needs to know how the donor has been involved with the organization so that they can discuss specific areas of progress and interest. In twenty minutes, you will not have time to check all of the different databases in the organization, so you print out what you have. As a result, you might be sending your boss or board member into a prospect meeting unprepared, and you might likely end up with missed opportunities similar to that in the previous example.

One thing that donors dislike is when organizations duplicate contacts with them. Donors view this as a waste of resources, and it makes them feel as if they are just a number, not a person. The more databases you have in an organization, the more likely it is that donors are going to receive duplicate letters, newsletters, phone calls, and so on. In the worst case, you might send two solicitations from the organization very close together, for different projects. This duplication signals to the donor that you do not know what your priorities are and that your organization is not well organized.

Consider all of the inefficiencies that multiple databases create. If you have an individual who is recorded on four separate databases, and the individual moves to a new address, that creates four different changes that have to be made in order to correct one mailing address. What happens if two of the managers of these databases are very diligent in making address changes, and two others are not? The donor might get things from you that are both mailed to the correct address and forwarded from the old address for a period of time. Again, this indicates to the donor that you are not organized.

Finally, the more data you have about a person in one location, the more effectively you can manage and analyze that data.

What steps should we take before purchasing a fundraising software system?

Step one is carefully defining all that you want your software to do. Think through the kinds of campaigns you run now and the kinds you might run in the next few years. Do you have a major gifts program or will you have one? If so, make sure you have your next steps and a way to track personal contacts with donors. If you do a lot of direct mail, you will want to be sure that you can easily segment the database for different kinds of mailings as well as easily generate reports to show you the results of each mailing.

Next you should consider the kinds of problems you are trying to fix with the software. What challenges are slowing you down in your day-to-day operations that you would like to address? Is your staff spending a lot of time rekeying information into different places in order to keep your records up to date? Do you have to export data into spreadsheets to generate the reports you need on a regular basis?

Look at your strategic plan and resource development plan and think about your short- and long-term goals. Look for a system that can grow with your program without a lot of additional costs. Gather ideas from staff and board members on what is needed. Rank your objectives in order of importance just in case you cannot immediately afford everything you need.

Create a list of functions and services you want from your software. Then develop an initial list of potential software providers. Visit software companies' websites. Collect information at conferences. Talk to other nonprofits in your community about the software that they use. Would they recommend it? What challenges do they face in using it? Do they have a fundraising program with as many as or more components than yours?

Once you have a list of vendors, make a short list of four or five that you think might be able to address your needs. Request information from them. Tell them your requirements for software and ask how their program addresses those.

Ask for references to organizations that are similar in size to yours. Be sure to get information on not just initial pricing for the software but also for training, upgrades, and ongoing service. Assume that you will have the program for up to five years and determine what will be the total costs over those five years.

It is very important to ask about how to convert your current data to fit this new system. What does that cost? How is it done? How long does it take?

Get a demonstration at your office of the top two or three packages. Be sure to do this in your office because that is where the program will ultimately be working for you—so the demonstration needs to work in your office too, right?

Make your decision, get a contract, be sure to ask about what happens if you find the system just doesn't work for you (after thirty days or so). Do you get any of your money back?

What are some pitfalls I should avoid when making a decision about fundraising software?

After many years of working with lots of different nonprofit organizations, we have some simple rules about fundraising software:

1. Do not buy a software system just because it is well known or popular in the market. One size does not fit all.
2. Do not build your own. You will waste countless hours doing something that has already been done by hundreds, if not thousands, of others.
3. Make sure at least two people at your organization are fully trained on how to manage the system to do what you need, and make sure one of those two people is you. Wouldn't you just hate to miss an important deadline or be unprepared for a significant meeting with volunteers because the one person who knew how to run the report you needed was out sick for the day?
4. If it takes someone with programming experience or a background in sophisticated database systems to generate fundraising reports, import or export data, or run your backup files, find another system or make sure these kinds of things are included in your support agreement.
5. Do not build your system around yesterday's technologies and fundraising strategies. If you will have to buy extra servers, computers, and software to

integrate the system with your online fundraising strategies, keep looking (unless you have a full time IT department at your beck and call). Online fundraising strategies are most effective when they are integrated with your offline fundraising strategies. To do so requires having one database from which you can send e-mail, generate letters, look up all giving records (including online gifts), and electronically input data collected online. Even if you are not heavily using the Internet today for fundraising, we have many reasons to believe you will be within the next few years.

What are some innovative ways that nonprofits are using technology?

Considering the speed at which our world is changing, we are always a little hesitant to write about innovative practices. They might be old news before our thoughts are published. But since nonprofits have not embraced innovations very quickly, much to the chagrin of numerous out-of-business dot-com companies, we will discuss some ideas here.

The newest area for many nonprofits is Internet-based programs, including e-newsletters, online donations, online special event management, and online advocacy. There is a growing trend to use the Internet in fundraising for processing donations, negotiating terms of major gifts, handling special event registrations, promoting special events, renewing memberships, and providing information to interested constituents.

How do I convince my board to invest in a website?

Some of your board members are reluctant to approve a budget for website development. They think that your constituents and donors will not interact with a nonprofit via the Internet. How can you convince them otherwise?

We know that lack of trust is a key reason that people might not give to a nonprofit. So creating an online environment that creates trust is critical. Here are some ways to build trust online:

- Have a privacy statement and post it online.
- Prominently display who runs your organization, both staff and board.
- Prominently display your organization's opt-in and opt-out options.

Another big way to build trust is to ensure that information sent to you via the Internet is secure. If you are going to collect donations online, make sure you can protect your donors' financial and personal information as it is being transmitted to you. Also, if you have any kind of form that you want people to send to you via the Internet, and if it will contain e-mail addresses and other sensitive information, you probably want to provide those forms on a secure page. To determine quickly whether a page on the Internet is secure or not, look in the browser address window for the *http* to change to *https*. Or look for the padlock icon on the bottom of your screen to appear closed.

Should we sell our list of e-mail addresses to generate revenue?

Generally we think it is a bad idea. The information that you have about your donors and supporters is one of the most valuable assets of your organization—so much so that we think it would be very difficult for you to develop a price for your list that would even come close to compensating your organization fully for this asset.

Keep in mind that most people hate spam (unwanted e-mail), and if they found out that your organization was the reason they had started receiving a lot of spam, you could expect a negative backlash.

If you plan on selling your list, especially with e-mail addresses, tell people up-front that you will, and give them an easy way to opt out of this. Additionally, look for some outside verification of the ethics of your system. For example, to aid organizations in their efforts to adhere to ethical principles of ePhilanthropy, the ePhilanthropy Foundation has created a self-test to allow nonprofits an opportunity to evaluate their online practices and to receive recommendations for improvements. This self-test seeks to identify problems or raise questions about the Philanthropy practices of a nonprofit organization or for a for-profit provider. To take the test, visit www.ephilanthropy.org/site/PageServer?pagename= selftest.

What are the laws that impact Internet-based fundraising efforts?

As of 2004, there are two sets of U. S. laws that impact Internet-based fundraising efforts. The first is the federal Can Spam Act. The second is state charitable registration laws.

States began regulating spam in 1997. Nevada led the way. Most state laws prohibit unsolicited commercial e-mail except with certain headers or other provisions such as the establishment of a preexisting relationship. California and Delaware now have the toughest antispam legislation. As of November 2003, thirty-four states had some form of antispam law. A summary of state laws can be found at www.spamlaws.com.

The federal Can Spam Act became effective as of January 1, 2004. "It requires unsolicited commercial e-mail messages to be labeled (though not by a standard method) and to include opt-out instructions and the sender's physical address. It prohibits the use of deceptive subject lines and false headers in such messages. The FTC is authorized (but not required) to establish a 'do-not-e-mail' registry" (www.ftc.gov/bcp/conline/pubs/buspubs/canspam.htm). So who do you think is the target of this law? Commercial spammers, hackers, and porno rings primarily.

Charitable registration laws also have an impact on Internet fundraising as well as on all forms of fundraising, including direct mail and personal solicitation. Not all fifty states require registration; all the rules regarding this topic can be found at the following link: www.nasconet.org/public.php?pubsec=4&curdoc=10.

As they relate to Internet fundraising, here are the current main points:

1. If your state requires you to register, you should register.
2. If you specifically target any of your fundraising activities (online or off) to individuals in another state that requires registration, you should register in that state.
3. If you are getting more than $25,000 a year from individuals in a state that requires registration, you should register in that state.
4. If you are getting gifts from more than one hundred individuals in a state that requires registration, you should register in that state.

Can you really raise more money via e-mail than you can via direct mail?

Whether or not you will make as much money e-mailing people as you would sending letters will depend on the following:

- The quality of your e-mail list
- Permission to e-mail the list
- Having people on the list indicate that they would like to receive information via e-mail
- The source of your e-mail list (if they are people who have been on your website and have asked to be contacted, then you will have very strong results)
- Your ability to make your case for support and create a sense of urgency
- Your strategy for soliciting via e-mail, which should include thank yous and second solicitations
- Your technology's ability to keep information up to date on your website and track your e-mail response rates and changes

Does every nonprofit need a website?

Yes, it is worth building an online presence and creating systems for donors to give and communicate with you online. It is also important to use a website as a means of communicating your mission and your stewardship practices to a larger audience. Many nonprofits cannot afford to print fancy annual reports and thus are not able to provide all of their constituents with information about their finances and impact. This same information can be communicated on a website very affordably.

Having a solid Internet strategy is almost like having an unlimited marketing budget. It allows for the personalization of hundreds, if not thousands of communications, at a fraction of the costs of other methods. And remember: personalization produces better fundraising results.

What are some key elements of a good nonprofit website?

First, it should explain your mission and provide pertinent information. Second, it should provide visitors with a way to interact with you and contribute to your mission. This goes so much beyond a "give now" button and can include offering a place to sign up for an e-newsletter, to volunteer, or to contact someone for more information. Third, it should provide information on your finances and the leadership of your organization, including your board and key staff members. Fourth, if you are seeking donations online, you need to make your case for support and create a sense of urgency. Fifth, it should give people a reason to come back on a regular basis. Sixth, it should be registered with various search engines. Seventh, it should provide for secure transactions and be in keeping with ethical and security issues.

What are the advantages of an e-newsletter, and how do we start one?

Because e-newsletters do not have to be printed and mailed with postage, they are less expensive than paper newsletters. Additionally, because they can be sent out almost immediately after being written, they can contain more recent news and information.

Because e-newsletters easily allow for personalization, you can create a special message to different segments of your constituency. For example, you could have a different e-newsletter for donors, volunteers, prospective donors, and major donors, each with a special message crafted to their interests.

E-newsletters are also easier for your constituents to share with their friends and associates. Consider what would happen if your organization sent a paper newsletter to me, and I saw something in it that I thought might interest some of my associates. There is very little chance that I will make photocopies of it and mail it to my associates. However, if I received an e-newsletter from your organization and wanted to share it with my friends, I could easily point, click, and distribute it to as many people as I thought would find an interest in it. As a result, everyone who gets one of your e-newsletters from me is getting an e-mail from someone that they know and trust, not some organization with which they are unfamiliar.

This aspect of the Internet makes it very possible to exponentially multiply the impact of the old fundraising adage that people give to people.

Summary

If you want to increase your fundraising program's effectiveness, embracing technology and mastering the latest trends will help significantly. Learn how to use e-mail to communicate with your organization's constituents. Know how to produce reports that show the impact of your fundraising programs. Build your knowledge of web-based tools. Not only will this help your fundraising program; it also will greatly improve your ability to reach more donors with your organization's mission. It will also improve your marketability as a fundraiser.

CHAPTER FOURTEEN

STEWARDSHIP:
SAYING THANKS PAYS DIVIDENDS

An often overlooked and important part of the fundraising process is stewardship. Most nonprofits will do a better job of identifying, involving, and soliciting donors than they will of "caring and feeding" prior donors. We often see too much focus on those who have not yet given and a lack of understanding that the best prospects are generally those who are already past donors. And we also find that most nonprofits understand only the most basic level of stewardship: sending thank you letters to donors.

However, stewardship from a fundraising perspective means conducting your business from both a donor perspective and an institutional perspective. In other words, practicing good stewardship goes beyond issuing receipts to donors and becomes a part of the culture of the organization. It is one of the most important responsibilities of a board.

An organization with good stewardship practices is open about how it works. Decisions are made according to the organization's procedures. Board members regularly review financial statements, and an annual audit is conducted. Donors are kept apprised of how philanthropic dollars are being spent to further the mission of the organization. And the organization maintains written policies and procedures about financial matters that would meet the scrutiny of any interested major donor. Policies about endowment spending, gift acceptance, campaign accounting, and conflict of interest statements for the board are but a few examples.

In this chapter, we further define stewardship and explore some of the implications of practicing good stewardship with real-life examples. You will find answers to the following questions in this chapter:

- What is stewardship?
- Who is responsible for stewardship?
- How do we effectively and ethically provide different recognition for donors who give different amounts?
- How should we thank our donors?
- What are some creative ways to recognize donors who give year-in and year-out?
- Do all gifts need to be acknowledged with a letter. Who should sign thank you letters?
- Do you have any suggestions on how we should contact donors to arrange thank you visits?
- When should pledges be acknowledged?
- What should we include in our year-end tax letters to donors?
- What should we include in our annual report?
- Is it appropriate to publish the names of donors without their permission?
- When a couple has given a gift, and since then one of the partners has passed away, is it appropriate to still list both of them within the first year of the passing?
- When a donor makes a gift anonymously, do you acknowledge the gift generally, even though you do not include it in any listings or programs?
- Who should get credit for the matching gift from a corporation?
- Our local newspaper has been especially supportive this year. We want to recognize them in a meaningful way. What would you suggest?
- What is a good way to recognize a major individual donor and further involve that person in our organization?
- How can we express our appreciation to our board members? Should we recognize event sponsors in our annual giving clubs?
- What is the most appropriate way to contact the donors who are behind on pledge payments?
- What are the stewardship policies my organization should have in place?
- What are some guidelines regarding donor surveys?
- Are there general guidelines for pricing named gift opportunities?

What is stewardship?

We have a simple definition. *Stewardship* is the process whereby an organization respects and protects its philanthropic support—its gifts and the donors who give them—in a way that validates the importance of philanthropy to the mission of the organization.

Stewardship involves promptly thanking donors, providing donors with IRS-required receipts, ensuring that the recognition of gifts is consistent with donor expectations, keeping accurate records of donors' gifts over time, designating and using donated funds as intended, issuing regular reports on the work of the organization, and, where possible, visiting personally with donors throughout the year.

A good stewardship program provides donors with receipts for their gifts, acknowledges gifts to donors, keeps accurate records of gifts that are made and the terms of the gifts, has written policies regarding what kinds of gifts are accepted and how they are recognized, has accurate financial records and can easily show both the sources and uses of funding, ensures that an annual audit is done of financial records, can show that the board regularly reviews and approves financial records, provides regular reports to donors on the use and impact of funds, and finally, ensures that all actions of the organization are such that we would not mind reading about them in the newspaper.

Who is responsible for stewardship?

The board of a nonprofit has the utmost responsibility. Staff should handle the operational side of stewardship, such as preparing letters, managing the donor database, organizing financial information and records, and, when appropriate, visiting with donors. The board should make sure the organization has a culture of openness, in personally thanking the organization's largest supporters, in regularly reviewing the organization's financial condition and keeping written minutes of its review, in ensuring there is an annual financial audit of the organization, and in making sure that all donors know how their funds are used.

A question from one of our clients helps to illustrate why both the staff and the board have responsibilities related to stewardship. Our client wrote to us as follows:

> We have partnered with three other colleges and accepted a grant from a foundation. The grant monies are split five ways: an equal sum to each college, and a collective sum for the administration of preresearch and postresearch discussions. It is widely believed that the money used for the collective group will be enough to satisfy the terms of the grant. Some argue the institution's portion can go to other things (like the annual fund). I argue that we are bound to adhere to the terms of the award because we accepted the foundation's offer— even if we do not really need to spend the money to accomplish the outcomes. Am I nuts? How do I have this conversation with my seniors?

In this situation, we would not recommend that the staff go directly to the board with this concern. However, that might become an option of last resort. Instead, in these types of circumstances it is better to initiate discussions with other staff members about the use of funds by starting with the person who has the best relationship with the donor. Start in the context of, "It is my understanding that we need to present a written report to the donor on the use of the funds. What should be contained in that report?" If this staff member is willing to disclose fully how the funds are being used then they have satisfied being good stewards. On the other hand, if they are secretive regarding the use of the funds, then there is a problem that needs to be addressed. Again, your best ally will be the person who initiated this grant and has the best relationship with the donor. The donor will not want his or her own reputation soiled as a result of the funds being misused.

How do we effectively and ethically provide different recognition for donors who give different amounts?

The purpose of recognition is to promote donors as examples to others and to challenge them to rise to higher levels of support. Gift clubs and societies are some of the best ways to recognize donors at different levels of giving. With gift clubs and societies, you can establish recognition programs related to levels of giving. For example, for your biggest donors each year, you could hold a special dinner. For donors at lower but still significant levels, you can give some kind of memento.

One great thing about gift clubs is that they help you create reasons for donors to increase their giving each year—to join a new gift society or club. You will need to look at some past giving records to determine how to set your giving levels. The highest level should be consistent with just a little higher than the annual giving of your best donors.

Establish that your gift clubs are for annual gifts only. Recognition for cumulative giving should have a different strategy. Annual giving clubs should be organized according to the nature of your constituency. For most organizations, $100 to $250 should be the floor for the lowest-level giving clubs. You can recognize gifts less than $100 as "Other Donors" or "Friends" in your honor roll of donors, but you need that $100 level as the first stretch point for donors.

The top level should be $10,000 plus. The pivot point is the $1,000 level. Whether you use one or two levels between $100 and $1,000 and between $1,000 and $10,000 depends on what makes sense for upgrading your donors. However, this is not a hard-and-fast rule. If you have a lot of donors who are giving more than $10,000 each and every year, and you are actively pursuing gifts of $25,000, $50,000, or more for annual support, then you might want to start a gift club over $10,000. But that should be your test: will there be a number of people in the higher gift club range, and are you going to pursue annual gifts strategically at these higher levels? Remember that the gifts need to be for annual support to qualify. You might have donors giving at higher levels, but their gifts might be for capital or endowment. There are other ways to recognize these restricted gifts.

How should we thank our donors?

The best thank you gifts for donors are things that have a connection to your services and really say thank you. You can, of course, purchase pens and other trinkets with your logo on them for relatively little money. However, while donors might find these useful, if they are not unique to your organization they will not help reinforce the connection the donor has to your organization.

Like most things in fundraising, the best ways of saying thank you are the most personal. If you have youth programs, for example, you could have some of the young people who participate in your programs write short notes to donors telling them how and why your programs are important to them. These notes (preferably the originals rather than copies) could be included with a thank you letter from you to your donors. Similarly, a photo of a group of young people holding a sign that is personalized could be effective. Each sign in the photos would be donor specific. ("Thank you [name of donor] for helping us grow.") This might be time consuming (especially in getting the parents' permission to include their children in these efforts). But with a digital camera and a color printer, your cost would be minimal, and your donors will appreciate the effort more than they would cheap trinkets.

Donors often complain that they never hear from charities except when the charities want money. Remember, people give to your organization because they want to improve the lives of those you serve. The best thing that you can give them in thanks is evidence that they are making a difference.

We created the following "ABCs of Donor Recognition" as helpful guidance for establishing recognition programs:

Appropriate: make the recognition appropriate to the gift. The IRS has rules regarding what a donor can receive from an organization. Make sure you are following these guidelines. Appropriate also means that a good old-fashioned thank you note is a wonderful donor recognition strategy. Listing donors in publications or on your website can also be appropriate strategies.

Beneficial: the recognition should encourage the donor and others to give and give more than usual. Creating special gift club levels that relate to the history of your organization or community and carry some prestige to them often do this. The recognition should also be beneficial to the organization in that it attracts other donors and doesn't cost more than it produces.

Consistent: recognition programs should not change often; nor should rules be changed for specific circumstances or individual situations. For example, gift recognition clubs should recognize those who give money rather than time or gifts in kind, who could be recognized separately.

Distinctive: a good recognition program is unique to your organization and its mission. A good example is a name-giving club in which the levels with names reflect the organization's mission. Some housing organizations use Master Builder, House Partner, and so on. A botanical garden uses orchards, daisies, and roses. A children's home uses angels and guardians; many organizations use gold, silver, and bronze or diamonds, rubies, emeralds; or president's council, trustee council, leadership council, or the name of a famous historical person, and so on.

What are some creative ways to recognize donors who give year-in and year-out?

A cumulative giving society is important for developing long-term relationships with your donors. You can have one society with multiple levels: $100,000 plus, $250,000 plus, and so on. If your records are sketchy in early years, you should issue your first roster of your cumulative giving society as a draft with a disclaimer that you have tried your best to include all past gifts. This will give your donors the opportunity to correct the record, and avoid rancor over omissions.

Do all gifts need to be acknowledged with a letter? Who should sign thank you letters?

A couple of years ago, we went to a wedding for a couple that we did not know very well. Because we are really good friends with the groom's parents, we also sent a present for the newlyweds. Six months went by, and we did not receive a thank you note from the bride and groom. So we asked the groom's parents about it, and they said, "We are sure they received the gift and appreciated it very much. They have just had so much to do since the wedding; we don't think they had a chance to write to everyone." You can probably imagine how this made us feel. Some people got written thank you letters. Others did not. As we did not, to this day, we wonder if the couple received the gift and why we were deemed unworthy of a thank you note.

Perhaps this is an extreme example of why providing a written thank you note to every donor is a good idea. It assures each donor that you received the gift and shows that you appreciate what he or she has done for your organization. Consider also that donors who give $250 or more will need written receipts for tax purposes.

You can, of course, have different forms of letters that are sent depending upon the size of the gift. For example, for your highest level of donor, you might personalize the letter completely and include recent organizational news and accomplishments along with a handwritten personal note. You might also call to personally thank any donor or one that gives in excess of a certain amount. Most organizations develop a tiered system for phone calls, personal notes, thank you letters, and signatures.

Ideally, the person who solicits the gifts should be the one who signs the thank you letter. Then some type of hierarchy is developed for who signs the official letter. For example, the board chair might sign letters to the largest donors, the campaign chair for the next group, the executive director for the next, and so on. For gifts above a certain level, many organizations send two thank you letters.

Do you have any suggestions on how we should contact donors to arrange thank you visits?

Let's say your organization has decided that you want to visit and thank personally all donors who contribute $2,500 or more during a year, but you are having trouble getting appointments with the donors. First, since you know that you want to visit higher-level donors, use that knowledge to affect how you handle those donors from the start. Specifically, call each of those donors when their original gift or pledge is first received and thank them. Share with them information about how donated dollars are being used. Ask them what motivated them to support your organization. Ask them just a little about themselves. Build rapport. You get the picture. Then, toward the close of the conversation, let them know that you would love to meet them. By doing this, you will build better donor relations whether or not you are able to visit them. You will be able to gather important information about the donor that could be very helpful in subsequent solicitations. And you will increase the likelihood that you will get the appointment when you call.

Second, recognize the donor's biggest fear about your visiting, and neutralize it. What is their fear? Naturally, it's that you will ask them for more money. How much money? Well, they don't know that either—and that is an additional point of discomfort. Let's face it: donors today are intelligent. And they know what your job is—to secure financial support. So if you know that you are not going to solicit the individual for a gift, then say so when you are making the appointment. "Mr. Jones, I would very much like to have the opportunity to meet you and to thank you in person for the generous support you have provided us. And I will make you a promise. While I'm there, I won't ask you for one penny. In fact, we won't even talk about money, unless you bring it up." If you get in under those conditions, you must honor your commitment. However, there is one thing you can and should ask your prospect. As you are concluding your meeting, ask if she or he will allow you to visit again when you are next in the area. Having had that first meeting, you will be in a much better position on your next trip to see about increasing that gift.

When you are setting appointments be as nonthreatening as possible. For instance, if you are trying to visit someone who lives out of town, the donor might feel really put on the spot if they know you are traveling just to see them. But you can call with plenty of advance notice and say, "I am going to be in the area for [a vacation, a meeting, and so on], and I wanted to know if I could have the opportunity to meet you. I would like to bring you the statistics from our last two years' work and show you how much your gift has helped us fulfill our mission." Or "I would like to share with you some of our tentative plans for the future and get your feedback on them before we move forward."

For those who are closer, instead of visiting them, you might wish to invite them to your facilities to show them what is going on. (This is easier to do if you have something new to show them.) For those who are reluctant to come on their own, consider having an event, or a thank you tour, and invite a number of donors. This way you and board members meet them and at the same time show them how their gifts are used

Finally, use your board development committee to help with either arranging the visits or paving the way for you to visit. Sometimes a phone call from the right volunteer can open doors that might be difficult for staff to open.

When should pledges be acknowledged?

Depending upon the size of the pledge and the payment, it is a great idea to acknowledge pledges promptly when they are made and to acknowledge payments on pledges when they are made. You should also send a pledge reminder thirty days before a pledge payment is due. Pledge acknowledgements should include the terms and conditions of the pledge and thank donors for any payments made with the pledge.

Acknowledging a pledge payment is another opportunity to thank your donors, provide on update on your activities, and show how their funds are being used.

Additionally, acknowledging a pledge payment is a good way to make sure additional payments are received. It shows that it is still important to your organization to receive those payments. Many organizations acknowledge pledge payments with language similar to, "thank you for your payment of $500 toward your campaign pledge of $2,500. Our records indicate that the remaining balance on your pledge is now $1,500. Thank you. Your gift and timely payments on this pledge are helping [name of organization] reach its goal of [dollar amount]."

When pledges are made through a United Way giving campaign, your practice might depend somewhat on the rules of the campaign organizer. That being said, we think it is a good practice to thank the donor when the pledge is first made and then thank the donor when you receive all payments on the pledge (since you will not be actually collecting all the payments directly).

What should we include in our year-end tax letters to donors?

Generally, you need to provide a receipt to any donor who gives $250 or more in one calendar year. A standard sample letter follows in Exhibit 14.1. Note that the sample includes a place to list any goods or services that your organization provided to the donor in exchange for their gift.

What should we include in our annual report?

An annual report is a great way to show donors and supporters how you are using their resources to accomplish the organization's mission. Annual reports can also be internal tools that help staff and board alike measure the organization's past accomplishments while contemplating its future directions. At a minimum, an annual report should include the following:

1. A letter from your board chair that hits the high points of the year and describes how donors helped make it all happen
2. Your mission statement
3. A listing of your board of directors, senior staff, and others who serve on important committees for your organization
4. Narrative on the impact of specific programs during the year and goals for the future
5. Financial information
6. Listing of your donors by gift club level or other designation that you choose

Be sure to show how much money was spent on programs versus administration and fundraising. If your financial statements are audited, include appropriate portions of the auditor's report. Graphs are also a good way to present a snapshot of your finances. More and more funders are going to ask for this kind of information before making a grant decision. Having it all in one place will make it easier for you to present it and include it in proposals.

EXHIBIT 14.1. SAMPLE END-OF-YEAR LETTER.

(Print on organization's letterhead.)

PLEASE RETAIN THIS LETTER FOR YOUR [TAX YEAR] TAX FILES

Date
Donor name
Address
City, state, zip

Dear [Name],

Thank you for your generous support of [name of organization]. We are grateful to acknowledge a gift for the [name] campaign. Federal tax regulations require donors to provide the IRS with written substantiation for gifts of $250 or more. According to our records, you have made the following contribution(s):

RECEIVED:

Check # 0000	MM/DD/YYYY	$ [amount]
Fair market value of goods and services	$ [amount]	
Check # 0000 MM/DD/YYYY	$ [amount]	
Fair market value of goods and services	$ [amount]	

If you have questions or concerns regarding this report, please contact [name, phone, e-mail]. Again, thank you for your support of [name of organization].

Sincerely,

[executive director or director of development]

We see more and more organizations with their annual reports online and think that this is a nice way to show people who are not as familiar with your organization that you are operating with integrity and have nothing to hide about your organization's finances.

If you have some special donors that you are trying to cultivate for bigger gifts, give some thought to how you might personally present the annual report to them. You could, for example, set up a personal briefing with them to deliver a copy of the report in person and discuss the main points with them. Or you could send an early copy with a personal note that says, "We want you to be one of the first to receive a preview of this year's annual report. I hope you will call me with your comments and questions once you have had a chance to review it."

Is it appropriate to publish the names of donors without their permission?

It is a generally accepted practice to list donors in an annual report, assuming that you are publishing other names too. Most donors who do not wish to be listed tend to let you know at the time of their gift that they want to be anonymous.

When it comes to how to list donors, consistency and personalization should rule. You might want to make your job easier by asking donors to define how they wanted to be listed. This can be done by providing a line on your pledge cards or business reply envelopes that reads, "For purposes of recognition, please list this gift as being made by [name]." This type of prompting will also help you identify anyone who wishes to remain anonymous.

When unsure, err on the side of formality. Keep some basic rules in mind. For example, remember that the man's first name always goes with his last name. So, an appropriate listing would be Jane and John Smith but not John and Jane Smith. If Jane and John have different last names, Jones and Smith respectively, and like to be listed as such, ladies are first. So the listing would read Jane Jones and John Smith or Mrs. Jane Jones and Mr. John Smith.

When a couple has given a gift, and since then one of the partners has passed away, is it appropriate to still list both of them within the first year of the passing?

A client sent us this example: Bob and Mary Stewart gave a gift within the last twelve months and indicated in writing that this is the listing they preferred for recognition. Bob recently passed away.

In these types of situations, you can take one of two directions:

1. You can use it as an opportunity to build your relationship with the surviving spouse (in this case, Mrs. Stewart) and call her. In the call, let her know how much you have appreciated the support that she and Mr. Stewart provided over the years (or last year if it was a one-time gift). You can express that you are sorry to learn of his passing and just wanted her to know that you will be remembering their combined generosity in this year's annual report.
2. You can simply list them both but use an asterisk and footnote to indicate that he is deceased. This is a practice used by many nonprofits.

When a donor makes a gift anonymously, do you acknowledge the gift generally even though you do not include it in any listings or programs?

Send the donors an acknowledgment letter thanking them for their gift and assuring them that the gift will only be attributed to an anonymous source. Be sure to include information in your letter about how their donation will help your organization achieve its goals. Also include a full description of the gift if it is a gift in kind.

The only reason you should not send a thank you letter is if the donors made their gift through a volunteer and told that volunteer that they did not want anyone else to know about it. In that case, the volunteer should send the thank you letter on behalf of your organization. You should still record the gift in your gift record system with an indication that it was an anonymous gift.

Who should get credit for the matching gift from a corporation?

Most nonprofits give hard credit to the corporation. *Hard credit* is where it is reported on fundraising and financial reports. But then the nonprofit gives *soft credit* to the employee whose gift initiated the match. When placing the donor in a giving society, many nonprofits include both soft and hard credit. This arrangement can be used with gifts from donor-advised funds of community foundations and similar entities.

Our local newspaper has been especially supportive this year. We want to recognize them in a meaningful way. What would you suggest?

To recognize the newspaper, you could do a brief article in your annual report that highlights what the newspaper did for you. Or write the publisher a personal letter expressing thanks for everything the newspaper has done. If there are particular newspaper staff members who were helpful, name them in your letter to the publisher and send a copy of the letter to the staff members that you name. If appropriate, you might consider a board resolution thanking the newspaper for its support. Newspapers also love to hear from advertisers, so be sure to ask prominent business owners on your board to also send thank you letters.

What is a good way to recognize a major individual donor and further involve that person in our organization?

Consider inviting her to your organization for a tour and lunch with your organization's leadership. Show her the impact her gift has made. Consider giving her a special certificate or other memento for her gift (but keep this in line with what you would do for other donors of similar amounts). Be sure to ask questions about her personal interest in your organization and look for ways to involve her further during these discussions. Listening to donors is more important than trying to sell them something. Be prepared to follow up quickly on any ideas or questions that they have during the tour and write a full report for your files to summarize and record the meeting.

How can we express our appreciation to our board members?

A good first step is to list your board in your annual report. Also, you should ask the chair of the board to write a personal letter to each board member that expresses thanks for what that individual board member has done for you in the past year. Consider having a portion of a board meeting that is dedicated to reviewing the accomplishments of the past year. This affords you the opportunity to highlight what individual board members have done to help the organization reach its goals and report on the participation level of the board in the prior year's annual fund.

Should we recognize event sponsors in our annual giving clubs?

We generally recommend that you recognize event sponsors as event sponsors and that you create specific ways of recognizing them that relate to the event. And we think this event sponsor recognition should be kept separate from annual giving level recognition. Why? Because when a company sponsors an event, some of their money is going toward expenses related to recognizing them along with expenses of the event. And they are generally receiving benefits for making their sponsorship (event tickets, advertising, and so on). On the other hand, someone giving to the annual campaign typically is giving to general unrestricted funds and receiving little if any benefit for their gift.

What is the most appropriate way to contact the donors who are behind on pledge payments?

Option one is to call the donors and tell them that you are new to the organization and are updating donor records. You noticed that they have an outstanding balance on their pledge to the capital campaign. Ask if that is consistent with their records. If they say yes, ask if a new schedule of payments would be helpful for them to contribute the balance of their pledge. If they say no, ask them what their records indicate. Make every effort to get your records and their records consistent and then ask how they would like to schedule contributing the balance.

Option two is to send a letter that basically says the same thing. Include with the letter a printout of your record of their pledge and pledge payments. If you hear nothing after a few weeks, give them a call. If you are not able to reach them by phone or mail, find the original team that solicited the donors for their gifts and ask the team to assist you in finding and contacting the donors. Try not to be shy or nervous about this task. People like to be reminded of their commitments.

What are the stewardship policies my organization should have in place?

At a minimum, most organizations should have written policies that address the following issues related to stewardship:

- Do you have a written procedure for acknowledging gifts?
- Do your recognition societies have written policies? In terms of eligibility, are pledges generally recognized when paid? Are planned gifts not recognized in the annual and cumulative societies? (We do not think they should be. Annual societies usually reflect the same time frame as your fiscal year. Annual gift societies are not restricted to annual fund gifts. You should recognize all outright gifts for all purposes.)
- Do you have a written procedure for advising donors on how to make gifts of stock?
- Do you have a gift acceptance and disposition policy? Do you have acceptance authority divided between staff and a gift acceptance committee? Does this policy provide for quid pro quo gifts? If you accept credit card and online gifts, do you provide for these in policy?
- Does your gift acceptance policy cover gifts of tangible personal property? Are these provisions cursory or detailed? Do they include disclosure provisions?
- Is your general rule that all stock gifts will be liquidated as soon as possible?
- Do you have a real estate gift acceptance policy? Does the policy cover environmental risk assessment? Is the policy clear on who pays for appraisals and other costs? Does the policy include disclosure requirements?

What are some guidelines regarding donor surveys?

First, be sure you know why you want to collect information. How will it be used? Will it be updated annually? Who will analyze the results? What will you do with it once you have it? Second, don't substitute a survey for face-to-face cultivation visits with your best prospects. Third, focus groups sometimes are more helpful than written surveys, as they give you an opportunity to gain more insight into donors' thoughts and comments. Finally, consider dividing your donors into two categories: those you will visit personally and those you will survey. If you have more than three thousand in your database, we suggest that you consider using a screening service to determine how many of your donors are good prospects for larger gifts and thus should be personally visited.

The people you visit should be people that you want to cultivate for additional (increased) support. Questions asked during personal visits should follow the natural flow of the conversation: what got you interested in our organization in the first place; are you aware of what we are doing currently; can I tell you about some of our plans for the future; and how can I contact you again for further discussion are all appropriate. The person making the visit should write up a call report that summarizes what was learned in the visit and what next steps should be taken with the donor.

In doing your mail survey (or, if possible, e-mail survey), include a cover letter that explains the purpose of the survey. We would not make the survey more than one page. Some questions to ask might include the following:

- How did you hear about our organization?
- Why did you choose to support our organization?
- Would you be interested in receiving our regular newsletter or additional information?
- Would you be interested in becoming more involved with our organization?

After you list these questions, leave room for comments and be sure to include a business reply envelope that encourages the survey participant to stamp it themselves but that can be mailed even if they do not stamp it.

Again, before doing any work on your survey, be sure to think through exactly what you hope to accomplish. Make sure you are crafting questions to reach your objectives.

Are there general guidelines for pricing named gift opportunities?

Typically, a starting point for pricing named gift opportunities is one-half of the cost of the project. However, this is only a starting point. Some areas are more visible than others and thus desire higher price tags. For example, a lobby might not cost a lot but might be a very visible area. We recommend that you consider these kinds of visible areas as being among the higher-priced naming opportunities—no matter what they cost. For example, we know of museums and hospitals that have priced their lobbies at five to six times the actual renovation and construction costs.

Other pointers on named gift opportunities include the following:

1. Your naming opportunities should be somewhat consistent with your Range of Gift Table. In other words, the size gifts you need to have a successful campaign coupled with the desirability of certain building areas—not the construction costs of each area—should guide how you determine your named

gift opportunities. For example, a lobby might not cost much to build, but if it will be a highly visible area, it warrants a high named gift level.

2. Have your campaign committee approve the named gift opportunities before the campaign begins.

3. Create a brochure that describes the named gift opportunities. Be sure to include the ones that are already taken, especially if the person naming the building has a compelling story to tell about why she is naming the building. Some organizations post their named gift opportunities on their websites. We do not recommend doing this until you have completed all of your face-to-face solicitations and have raised at least 90 percent of your goal.

4. Begin using the brochure in face-to-face solicitations. Give your solicitor guidelines about using the named gift opportunities in solicitations. "No negotiations" should be the number-one guideline.

5. Once you have completed all of your face-to-face solicitations, you might consider a broader-based solicitation method that encourages potential donors to participate in a "buy a brick"-type program. These work best when you have at least two different levels for buying a brick and have a very specific solicitation strategy—such as IDC's Phone/Mail Program, which involves a series of letters or e-mails followed by a series of phone calls.

Summary

Stewardship is all about two things: doing what is right and documenting what you do. It is about developing an institutional culture of transparency, efficiency, and effectiveness in your work.

There is a *60 Minutes* rule of stewardship. Imagine that someone comes into your office and says, "The people from *60 Minutes* are here and want to talk about how we do things." If you welcome them, you have a good stewardship program. If you are running for the window, it might be time to get the organization's stewardship act together.

Finally, remember that stewardship is the first step in the next solicitation, not the last step in receiving the prior gift.

CHAPTER FIFTEEN

PUTTING IT ALL TOGETHER

At the end of the day, your ability to thrive as a fundraiser depends more on your view of yourself and your role than on any other factor. The fundraiser with a high likelihood of success sees himself or herself in the following roles:

- An educator, not a salesperson
- A facilitator and supporter of the involvement of others, not a one-person show
- Someone who offers people the ability to make an impact on the world, not a hired gun or a solicitor begging for money
- A passionate individual who is making a difference with his or her own life, not someone working week to week for a paycheck
- An ethical practitioner of solid fundraising principles, not a professional eager to do whatever it takes to meet this year's fundraising goals
- A professional who is always learning, not someone who is shying away from new technologies and tools
- A positive, proactive solution provider, not a problem finder
- An effective communicator, both verbally and in writing
- Someone who knows the principles of fundraising and knows that there is no such thing as a situation so unique that the principles do not apply

Why is your self-perception so important? Because so much of your job has to do with educating and influencing others. For example, you might have noticed that many of the questions in this book were about what a fundraiser should tell the boss or board members about some idea. Whether it is an idea related to the big corporations, the New York foundations, or the Forbes 400, we have all spent too much time chasing the unattainable donor.

You can avoid these discussions by embracing your role as fundraising educator to all of those in your organization who can influence the success of the development program. Take every opportunity you have—board meetings, staff meetings, personal meetings with volunteers and board members—to educate your constituency about the contents of this book. Also, try to make the word *unique* a joke in your organization. This will keep everyone focused on following proven fundraising principles.

Do not expect to be perfect in a job situation and know that you might get bitten with the "grass is always greener on the other side" perception that hits all too many fundraisers. If you are contemplating changing jobs, be sure to do the following:

- Evaluate the person you will be reporting to and ensure that she or he understands and supports a strong development program.
- Believe in the mission of the organization. Every person will have challenges, and the more you appreciate and believe in the organization, the easier it will be to persevere.
- Evaluate the board's commitment to giving and getting funds for the organization. Two simple questions might save you a lot of heartache or find you a great position: (1) Does your board have 100 percent personal giving to the annual fund? (2) Could I review the minutes of your last two board development committee meetings?
- Thoroughly review the development office budget and make sure there are adequate resources to accomplish the prescribed objectives.

Finally, we know that in today's world, virtually all fundraising professionals will encounter ethical issues some time in their career. The best policy to follow in evaluating an ethical dilemma is to ask the question, *If the situation were to appear in local newspapers, would we be comfortable with our actions?* When tough topics such as values of in-kind gifts, named gift opportunity amounts, or potential misuse of insurance programs become potential ethical issues, use the newspaper question as your acid test for ethical decision making.

We thank you for reading this book and hope that it will improve your life and the life of those organizations you choose to serve in a positive and lasting way.

REFERENCES

Chapter Five

Brown, M. (ed). *Giving USA 2004*. Indianapolis, IN: AAFRC Trust for Philanthropy, 2003.

Chapter Eight

Hall, H., and others. "Giving Slowly Rebounds." *Chronicle of Philanthropy*, 2004, *17*(2), 26.

Chapter Ten

Alexander Haas Martin & Partners. "So You Want to Have an Endowment Campaign," 1999.

Havens, J., and Schervish, P. *Millionaires and the Millennium: New Estimates of the Forthcoming Wealth Transfer and the Prospects for a Golden Age of Philanthropy*. Boston: Social Welfare Research Institute at Boston College, 1999.

Stehle, V. "Charities Can Expect $1 Trillion from Transfer of Wealth Researcher Estimates." *Chronicle of Philanthropy*, 1998, *10*(19), 30.

Chapter Thirteen

"Dean Presidential Campaign Raises $3.6 Million Online." www.directmag.com/ar/marketing_dean_presidential_campaign/ (accessed June 1, 2004).

Iwata, E. "Tsunami Donors Creative in Giving." *USA Today*, Jan. 18, 2005, p. B1.

Lagace, M. "How Nonprofits Use the Internet to Get Ahead." *Harvard Business School Working Knowledge*. hbswk.hbs.edu/item.jhtml?id=4006&t=nonprofit (accessed May 2, 2005).

THE AUTHORS

G. Douglass Alexander is chairman of Alexander Haas Martin & Partners, one of the nation's leading full-service fundraising consulting firms. He is also chairman of MaGIC, (Major Gifts Identification and Consulting), a database research firm that provides computerized screening; and chairman of FundraisingINFO.com, the nation's leading Internet-based consulting firm. As the founder of five companies, Alexander has been an entrepreneur in providing fundraising services to nonprofit organizations since the 1970s. During this time, he helped nonprofit organizations raise billions of dollars.

Doug was born in Memphis and grew up in Mississippi and New Orleans before moving to Atlanta. He was an All-America high school basketball player at Cross Keys High School and an All-America at Oglethorpe University. He received an MBA from Georgia State University.

Doug resides with his wife, Kristina Carlson, in Atlanta and on their farm outside of Oxford, Mississippi, and has one daughter, Elisabeth Alexander Johnson.

Kristina Carlson has spent virtually her entire life nonprofit fundraising. She began as a young woman stuffing envelopes to raise money for several national organizations (where her father was development director). After graduating from Oral Roberts University, she joined one of the nation's leading fundraising consulting firms, Ketchum, directing capital campaigns. Her experience also includes work as a development director and major gift solicitor (securing gifts up to $15 million).

In 1999, Kristina helped found FundraisingINFO.com (FRI), an Internet-based fundraising consulting company. As president of FRI she has provided answers to hundreds of fundraising questions submitted to Ask Bee, and she has created Internet-based fundraising training and consulting services for Boys & Girls Clubs of America and the Association of Healthcare Philanthropy.

Kristina holds an M.S. degree in Community Economic Development from the University of Southern New Hampshire. She has lead more than three hundred workshops on fundraising since the year 2000 and was one of the first in the fundraising industry to be named an e-Philanthropy Master Trainer by the national ePhilanthropy Foundation. Kristina lives in Atlanta, Georgia and Water Valley, Mississippi with her husband, Doug Alexander.

Index